We Aren't Who We Are

How to Become

By

Dustin Ogle

Edited by Susan Strecker.

Printed by Countersign Publishing LLC, in the United States of America.

First printing, 2024.

Countersign Publishing LLC

507 N Buckeye St.

Kokomo, IN, 46901

www.dustinogle.com

CONTENTS

INTRODUCTION

If you were a wizard, would you know it?

I once saw a man stand over a dying woman and bring her back to life. He wore a strange outfit and wielded wands, potions, and instruments. Occasionally, he spoke in a foreign tongue that only he and his disciples understood. His congregation and apprentice stood near him. They offered whatever kind of support he needed. The Woman's life was saved.

Her version of what happened is that she had a heart attack. The doctor and surgical team performed a successful triple bypass. Both descriptions are accurate. That version sounds less magical or mystical and feels less amazing. But it isn't. We have an interesting way of assigning a higher value for what we don't understand or can't explain functionally or scientifically.

As soon as we learn how something works and can describe it, it tends to no longer feel as special or magical. But, if you think about it for a second, that notion is preposterous. But we do it with so many things in our world and with ourselves. Doing something incredible that takes great skill doesn't always feel special to us because we expect that outcome and know exactly how it happens. The vast amount of intentional learning and experience toward proficiency in a skill makes us very familiar with every little intricacy involved. By the time we become accomplished at using an ability, the feeling of executing an action with it isn't surprising to us. Contrarily, the experience is more expected and practiced instead of unfamiliar and astonishing. But it's worth noticing that we are doing amazing things every day and can do more in the future.

From my observation and many conversations with people, most of us believe that our best work, which expresses our strongest talent, would feel like a complicated overcoming or a surprising discovery. However, the reality is that our greatest abilities and most accomplished skills are the things that feel the easiest to come by and are the most obvious to us from our unique conscious experience.

To feel just how incredible your abilities are, you need to look at what skills seem easy to improve and obvious to you. Give those pursuits a higher priority and value. Then, push yourself to develop and learn about what greater things you can do with them. The more knowledge and skill we have, the more effective we become at performing our magic in the world. Your greatest power will not surprise you, even if you happen to feel like it should be. It will, however, make an impact, impress the hell out of other people, and create value for you to cash in on.

We see this surprise superpower as a motif in movies all the time. A character discovers or gains an extraordinary power that he accidentally starts using and has no idea how or why it works. That does seem incredible, and the function of the motif is to elicit a feeling from the audience. It taps into that feeling because we sense that something like that is possible. That sense is correct. Self-discovery is possible for us. Something exceptional inside of us is waiting to be unlocked, and we know it.

In reality, our individual special abilities don't feel strange to us. They feel natural. And our proficiency in using them comes from developing skills. If you work diligently and intentionally, you can turn your talents into special powers. I mean <u>special powers</u> in a strict sense of the definition. <u>Special</u> – "better, greater, or otherwise different from usual." <u>Powers</u> – "The ability to do something or act in a particular way, especially as a faculty or quality." A unique quality different than usual is your most valuable contribution to the world and is your special power.

Some people use their special powers to improve their lives and our world. We often call them and their accomplishments successful, amazing, and incredible. Many others spend their lives developing skills that they don't have a natural aptitude for to become more "well-rounded." Then, there are those who find their way to some version of an apathetic existence of not developing themselves much at all. Each path is a decision comprised of choices, whether we are aware we are making them or not.

"I am not what happened to me; I am what I choose to become." – Unknown.

We Aren't Who We Are gives a pragmatic approach and practical prescriptions to intentionally decide your path through action. It focuses some on *how* we work and primarily on *what* to do about it to get desired results rather than explaining *why* things are the way they are. This is a user's manual for ourselves since we didn't get one when we were born. Surprisingly, we are taught very little about how we function pragmatically. We don't need to completely know why something works to learn how to use it. And it is so much more fun and impactful to experience the discovery of the incredible feeling of why you exist for yourself rather than have someone like me try and poorly explain it.

Learning to operate yourself doesn't require you to understand your deep mechanics or their complicated existential implications like psychology, anatomy, neuroscience, spirituality, etc. Just like driving a car, it doesn't require you to understand its complicated mechanics to use it properly either.

Such is the same with oneself. We must learn to expertly operate our human selves. Leaving the political ideologies, existential beliefs, and religious dogmas in your back pocket is essential to learning how to drive yourself at the basic functional level so you can be objective and open. Pull those things out of your pocket if you want to, like a guide to help you decide where to go and what route to take once you are fully operational.

You can be shockingly successful in a surprisingly short time if you choose to be. You are already awesome. You just probably aren't exuding and experiencing your full potential. Together, we will realize your potential, learn how you really function, and execute intentional authority over that functionality to achieve incredible results. You will learn to self-engineer and pilot yourself as one machine made of body and mind working in effective harmony.

Once you start this approach, you will be surprised to discover just how accessible positive change is. You may experience an overwhelming cocktail of relief, excitement, grief, and hope. Be prepared to feel like a child in the world's mystery again, and then the zeal of inspiration like it's the first time. You will hardly believe the powers you have possessed this whole time as you are wielding them to reshape the world around you.

We are malleable. *We Aren't Who We Are* will show how we can change around 80 percent of what we call our "self" and why that is necessary to get new results. Leo Tolstoy pointed out, "Everyone thinks of changing the world, but no one thinks of changing himself." The truth is that a change in results will always be accompanied by a change in self. Simply putting the horse before the cart and seeking to change oneself first will pull the positive results along behind you quickly and steadily.

Our "self' is what we think of as our essential being that makes us different from other people. It includes the persona and identity that we craft and present to ourselves and others. We can change most of the characteristics that define us. I can show you how to positively cultivate your personality traits, abilities, likes and dislikes, motivations, self-image, and perception of life. We can change most of those things and more with one methodology.

We have a self-sustaining mechanism that entices us to change very little and cling to our perceptions and expectations. The mechanism is complicated, but I don't believe that positively affecting it is. The mechanisms and patterns that inhibit you can be altered to assist you. We now know it's possible to change our thought patterns and even alter some of our biology to our benefit. I believe the methods I present in the coming chapters are the best way to do this.

Our thoughts make proteins and electromagnetic and neuroendocrine signals while creating new neural pathways, and that all influence our many biological systems and epigenetic expression. Your thoughts exist in the material world, and they are mighty. Your mode of thinking doesn't just season your perspective; it assigns your interaction with meaning and instructs your body, including what you are able to sense from the outside world. It is impossible to change anything inside or outside of you without changing who you are to some degree. That is why we will focus on becoming skilled and intentional at changing who we are to get positive results.

Every morning, we program our experience with memories, ego data, and symbol affirmations. Your experience likely consists of waking up, and thoughts begin, remembering who you are, how you are supposed to feel, and who you imagine yourself to be. We instantly rebuild our "reality". It can feel like we are who we are, we do what we are able to, and we are difficult to change. Well, that is simply incorrect; there are other options I will show you and reasons you will be compelled to explore them.

We self-engineer our perception of reality. I believe around 80 percent of it must be created imaginatively and re-created constantly. We do this by interacting with our memory and imagination in our thoughts, and when we get a stimulus from outside ourselves via sensory perception, we try to fit it neatly into expectations and narratives. And we try to align it with the finite truth that persists everywhere by investigating for conformational evidence in some way. Your experience of the world around you is happening inside you, however. You aren't discovering reality outside of you nearly as much as you are creating it in your mind. Most of the other 20 percent isn't coming from the "outside" world either. It comes from a deeper part of your mind and body that you are less conscious or unconscious of. Some of that can also be changed; it just takes a little longer. A small percentage of who we are within that 20 percent is strongly biological. That small percentage is essential but still mysterious or widely misunderstood. But that isn't problematic on its own.

So, let's go back to the 80 percent of you that you can change easily. I'm talking about the thoughts that you are making and the actions you are taking in every moment. That amount of change could bring about wild results very quickly. When you make changes on the inside, they have consequences on the outside. The quality of your internal changes will determine the quality of your external results. Positive results are what we are after, and positive changes in our "self" are how we get them.

Look at it from this angle. If a mechanical engineer wants to change the output of a machine, she would be optimistic if she could rework the design by 2 – 4 percent overall. She would call an 80 percent redesign a completely new machine that could create almost any desired output. Even if I'm wrong and overestimating the 80 percent, we only need a fraction of that to dramatically change the quality of our output, especially through incremental improvement. You can change almost any amount of who you are immediately. And you have permission to do so even though it may feel as if you don't.

As you follow through the approach and methods of *We Aren't Who We Are,* you will find out exactly what I mean by this and how to make your desired changes pointing toward success. You may only need a small change or tweak to accomplish what you want, or you may decide you need an overhaul. This approach will also help you gauge how much change you need and calibrate your ability to assess that.

Many Buddhists describe this process of recreating ourselves as reincarnation. We often think about that as being born again after we die. That isn't the only concept of understanding reincarnation. Another is describing that a person is reborn constantly. You are not the person you were five years ago, five days ago, not even five minutes ago. You aren't your things, you aren't your situation, and you definitely are not your past. Your body isn't even made of the same cells as a few years ago. Why be reborn as almost the same person every day, especially if you aren't delighted with that person's results? Because we don't know how to influence that rebirth with authority and method. So, we are afraid and skeptical. Old patterns feel reliable and comfortable. You can confidently become whoever you want to be as soon as you know how. You will also be dumbfounded by how much the environment outside of you changes as a result.

Once this knowledge and how to use it becomes your reality,

you will irrefutably see for yourself that things don't happen to you. You happen to you and things. There will be no point in avoiding responsibility anymore.

You are a wizard. You are a self-engineer. You always have been. A great friend and brilliant man once said to me, "Publishing anything can be arrogant. You are suggesting that you have something special to say that other people need to hear." That has always been a daunting concept for me. This is the first time in my life, plagued with critical thinking, much writing, and intense living, that I believe I have something special to say. It's special because I have proof and encouragement that people need and want it. Further, I think the timing is right, and I'm obligated to communicate it to an audience I don't know personally. It feels urgently critical for many people to hear this right now. I believe this mainly because I am a survivor of unbelievable failures and remarkable successes. I know both paths very well.

Fifteen years ago, at the age of twenty-eight, I took the leap of quitting my good-paying job and started my first business. I have been the master of my universe ever since and have owned ten successful companies and counting. It can suck so much more than I thought possible. It can also be so much more incredible than I imagined. You can learn from me and advance into the wonderful parts of mastering your universe, whatever is like for you.

I am writing this first for myself. Writing is how I best think and develop my ideas and plans and map things out. This book will be a reference for me whenever I get lost again, as I certainly will. It is based on a lifetime of learning, listening, observation, and experimentation.

I got into a fair bit of trouble as a boy. I was significantly underqualified to handle emotions. I trained and competed as a wrestler year-round from nine to eighteen. I was a hopeless failure who persisted until I became a formidable champion. I learned the power of discipline and incremental improvement. Those years permanently installed an approach to life that saved me from a future of more debilitating emotions, poor choices, destructive behaviors, and, subsequently, terrible results.

My general approach to life is to have a strategy, work hard, walk calmly through the pain and discomfort, and win or lose, always accepting responsibility for the process and outcome. There are no fallback plans. I am alone every time I walk on a proverbial wrestling mat to face an adversary (usually myself). This was my way of viewing the apparent resistance of the world. While it may sound unappealing, don't judge too quickly. It is remarkably reliable. It may be a simplistic approach that doesn't properly use the benefits of support, but it led me to develop a unique perspective with many great lessons to share with you about just how much a person is capable of and how. By adopting the concepts and methods I discovered, you can avoid much of the friction and suffering I experienced along the way.

I worked my way through college, only stopping by my 300-square-foot apartment to either party or sleep. After completing a four-year run as an undecided major with a three-year break in the middle as a professional musician, I finally decided on an English major. My fifth year was all research, critical thinking, and formal writing. The day after I graduated, I quit my job and started my first business. From there, it gets wild, but that's another story.

I have since started and developed a dozen companies and many nonprofessional but valuable personal projects. I spent eight years learning to be a father before my lovely wife, and I decided to have a second child. I sold four companies to free up my time and attention to be the best father possible. That was eight years ago, and for thirteen years now, I am always grateful to have the chance to put a tremendous amount of time and effort into fatherhood. It never feels like a sacrifice to me.

I also spent the last twenty years on developmental personal projects such as learning songwriting, piano, guitar, a second language, chemistry in product formulation, photography, writing, research, mycology, carpentry, IT, philosophy, and many others. People often comment that there is nothing I can't do, and they don't know where I find the time to do everything. Of course, there are still loads of things I suck at and am ignorant about, but I have found a way to be absolutely riveted to become proficient at one thing after another continually for most of my life. I have also trained, developed, and employed thousands of other people. I have had the pleasure of meeting and interacting with a tremendous number of people. I have always been passionate about learning and working within every facet of my businesses. I believe that this type of inspired living can be created by anyone for their own life in their own way. I will show you how I do it, and hopefully, you can use my methods as your launchpad.

I always try and observe the dance of humanity from many perspectives. I have studied this reality as a scientist, poet, philosopher, salesman, property developer, maintenance man, web and social developer, CEO, negotiator, HR, musician, accountant, many at the same time, and on and on…. And I have created the environments in which I have done these things.

My favorite endeavor was bartending at bars and live music venues that I created with fantastic help. For better or worse, I am responsible for selling around $40 million and counting in alcohol from ten different establishments, one drink at a time. Much of the sales were at dance clubs or live performance venues, with socializing being the draw and aim. My first, second, and biggest of these venues was named The Social Experience. Experience was what we were selling more so than food or alcohol. My oldest friend and then-business partner, Ben, and I used to joke that it was more of an ongoing social experiment.

There is something fascinating and dangerous about studying people and participating with them as a bartender. I have engaged with an enormous survey of people from all walks of life who get chemically influenced to lower their inhibitions and unfold themselves right in front of me. I have witnessed the best and worst of people and could see the same in myself. I have been responsible for managing the unpredictability and studying the consistent emerging patterns of thousands of people coming together under the influence of booze and music. I also engaged with them as a listening ear, matchmaker, advice giver, friend, authority, physical security, caregiver, inspirational speaker, etc. I was at my best when I focused on precisely what a person needed from me and why. It was rarely the drink they needed.

I am writing this secondly for my family. This is a standard I have used many times before that I find helpful. I do things better for them than I do for myself. For my incredible wife, Lindsey Ogle, who has been my best friend and an essential partner for me in many ways. Her ability to survive my failures and successes while staying committed to encouraging and inspiring me is nothing short of miraculous. Our conversations and inquiry into the truth on this great adventure of life together have provided me with deep insight from her uniquely ethereal feminine perspective. Thanks to her, I'm certain that my perspective is richer, more balanced, and more sensitive. I hope this book serves to further inspire our united development in leading our family, businesses, and community together.

Also, for my children. I'm aware that some of the things in this book will attract much criticism and are, in many ways, counter-cultural and counter-popular narratives. But I must use what I believe to be true to positively impact the world my daughters will live in when they leave my house. Also, I hope they will take much of what I have learned and accomplish more than I have in every way. This is every father's hope, I think. Hope is cool, but I like having a plan and executing it.

My brother, Nathan, died a couple of years ago. We were very close. He struggled with life for a long time, especially after returning from war. Despite my efforts, I was never able to help him enough. I won't repeat that failure.

Finally, I am writing this for anyone I can help directly or indirectly. I am writing this for the people who will be critical and disagree with my methods and ideas so that they can hone their thoughts better and inspire further progress of their own. We are entering a post-corrupt enlightenment period in the West, plagued with propaganda and a war of persuasive ideas. These ideas are diseases to one's true nature, peace, and unity. I hope there will continue to be an influx of people seeking a way out of the possessions of bad ideas and finding ways to rely on themselves and the truth. I hope that this book assists them more than anything.

When I was a college student, one of my professors discovered that I was an aspiring musician and songwriter, as I was giving him an excuse for missing class. He surprised me by saying, "Your talents are always more important than your other obligations. Your talents are your obligations to contribute to the world, and there isn't anything more important than that." At that moment, I had a strange new feeling that not sharing the products of my talent was selfish.

I thought about that over the next semester and decided to reach out to him. In an odd twist, I discovered that he died shortly after he said that to me. I have thought about that many times in my life. I have been much more inspired to share my talents with others than I would have. It may have been the best advice I've ever received, and I will pass it on to you now.

"Your talents are always more important than your other obligations. Your talents are your obligations to contribute to the world, and there isn't anything more important than that."

Now, what to do about it . . .

OPENING THE DOOR

You are wrong about many things. Your ignorance negatively affects your thinking. Your flawed thoughts corrupt your actions. Your results and experience in life are much lower than they could be.

How did that make you feel? Think about it for a minute, please.

Regardless of your level of success in life, if there is no chance you will ever accept that statement, there is no reason to read on. If you are open to this possibility, you are in the right place.

We should all accept that we are wrong about many things. A profound observation often accredited to Einstein is, *"We cannot solve our problems with the same thinking we used when we created them."* We have trouble being objective about ourselves, understandably so. We are in our experience, so it's difficult to look at ourselves from the outside. This is why solutions to other people's problems often seem obvious to us but not to them. We are also blind to some of our solutions and improvements.

We need to be a bit suspicious of ourselves. Notice that we can be stuck in a problem that we are failing to solve, but for some reason, we think we know the solution even though it doesn't seem to be working. We are even dismissive of new and different ideas that others may offer to solve the problem. We get emotionally attached to our ineffective strategy sometimes. That is the thing to be suspicious of.

Here is an example. I was recently assembling a rack to display house plants, and I was having trouble getting a bolt to start. I couldn't get a good angle, and the bolt kept cross-threading and getting stuck. My eight-year-old daughter noticed and suggested it wasn't the right bolt. I knew it was the right bolt; only one size was available. So, I flipped it around and tried a dozen more times after that before I finally surrendered and admitted that I didn't know what was wrong. As soon as I surrendered, I looked closely and learned that there were, in fact, two different types of bolts that were very close in diameter but just different enough to never fit in the wrong nut.

The solution was obvious to my daughter with her keen young eyes and outside perspective. However, I dismissed her suggestion and kept failing at forcing my ineffective strategy. I didn't need a better angle; I needed a different bolt. First, I had to learn that there was a different bolt. That meant I had to change my feelings to desire a solution more than prove my first decision correct. I was unconsciously more interested in being right than being effective. This is a simplistic example, but we often do a similar thing with big, important issues. One principle change of thinking that is effective for me is to try to be less suspicious of other people's ideas and more suspicious of my own when considering myself. I will likely be less objective.

We often don't have the best answer, but we act as if we do. We try to convince ourselves that there is just some condition or circumstance in our way. Well, yes, there is. We are in our way. The best way to get the answers is to get out of the way. Admit to ourselves that we are wrong and don't have the answers we need; also, we may be on the wrong path to finding them. This is the most difficult part for some reason, even though it's the most obvious and straightforward thing to do.

Here is a heuristic (a hands-on interactive way of learning something for yourself). Most of what I'll be showing you in *We Aren't Who We Are* will be a heuristic process or method. Please actually do these activities so you can get that experience. I believe that you are your greatest teacher, and experiential learning is the deepest and most impactful. The activity is to let go of your ego and your beliefs for a moment. Find a mirror, look yourself right in the eyes, and say, *"I am wrong about some things, and I don't yet know what actions will get me where I want to be."*

Then, take a few breaths. You'll notice that you don't start bleeding and die when you do this. Your ego may die a little, and that may hurt your feelings for a moment.

On the contrary, it feels good as soon as we are open in this way. A heavy shadow lifts from our shoulders and minds. Stress and pressure melt away. Feelings of honesty and clarity set in. And it becomes easy to find the shift in perspective we need. A door appears that you simply couldn't see before. That is the magic of discovering your ignorance.

Talking to yourself is an incredible tool. I'll get to more on that later, but for now, keep it to that one statement and remain open. Be advised that you never want to be negative or dishonest when speaking to yourself. There is nothing wrong with saying, "I don't know." On the contrary, it is the supreme type of wisdom. Being aware of our own ignorance is the same wisdom that Plato wrote about in his accounts of Socrates in the work *Apology*.

The mechanism we have seems to function by searching for where we are ignorant, allowing us to discover new possibilities and information available. But not searching for our ignorance lets our ego take over and convince us that our limited information must be complete and necessary to defend as such. So, new possibilities and information become perceived as a threat. The key to opening magical doors is searching for and finding your ignorance. No, you don't have to tell everyone when you find your ignorance, but you better damn well learn to tell yourself, or you're screwed. When you believe you are right and your ideas are complete, you are in a self-made prison of the mind that cannot be escaped until you kill that belief.

"The knowledge of error is the beginning of deliverance." – Epicurus.

You are always in exactly the right place in your experience, even when it's going poorly, especially then. When you notice that you feel like you are in the wrong place or a bad situation, that realization is the thing you should give your attention to. Problems and dire circumstances aren't coincidental misfortunes as they often seem to be; they are opportunities once you make them purposeful and take action. That realization of being in the wrong place or emotional state is the discovery you need and is the reason you are there. Notice that your judgment alone decides that your circumstances are unfavorable for the action you would like to take. That makes it the right place to enact change. That feeling of "things are going wrong" is more useful to understand as "I am making some kind of mistake, and there is an opportunity here." The process of intentionally doing something different to change what is happening to you is the process of learning from your mistake.

However, if you don't give that realization attention and seek to take new action, you will continually find yourself in that undesirable place. This is how a call to change is delivered to you. Ignoring it will make it keep coming. There are no permanent destinations, only good or bad directions. Here are a few translations of this core idea from Marcus Aurelius. *"The impediment to action advances action." "The obstacle is the way". "What stands in the way becomes the way."*

I don't have all of life's answers, but I can tell you how I found enough of them to get results and how you can turn problems into solutions. And it's a truly meaningful experience. You may not like discovering what you are doing wrong; I sure didn't. Be suspicious of this. If you want to be more successful and have a better life experience, you must grab onto the idea that you want to discover where you are failing or uninformed about yourself. This is what you need! If you go through this text only looking for positive confirmation about the things you already think, you will find some, nobody will care, and you won't learn anything useful for yourself.

In contrast to our ignorance, it is perplexing that we all already know some things we should be doing to get where we want to be in life. But sometimes, we don't do them, at least not consistently enough to get results. We often choose to engage in actions that take us further from where we want to be. When we are at our worst, we are apathetic. Apathy is the word we use logically, scientifically, and medically to describe giving up on trying at life. Subclinical apathy (some apathy but not enough to be a medical condition) can be identified and measured in 35 percent of the general healthy population (see *Distinct subtypes of apathy revealed by the apathy motivation index).*

Apathy is the worst kind of meaningless existence and is an open invitation to tyranny. It can lead to a dangerous complacency. When individuals become apathetic, they often lose the will to engage in the processes of social life and lose sight of their principles, values, and ethics. This disengagement can create a power vacuum that those with authoritarian tendencies can exploit. Apathetic individuals are less likely to question the actions of those in power, less likely to hold them accountable, and less likely to advocate for their rights and the rights of others. They lose their fighting spirit.

Tyranny thrives on apathy. When people stop caring about their ideas, freedoms, and the well-being of their communities, it creates an environment where those in power can act without opposition or accountability. They can use propaganda, intimidation, and other tactics to manipulate and control, eroding freedoms and consolidating their own power.

Many people want to improve themselves. They will say things such as being in better physical shape, having more money, having a better relationship, and maybe working on their personal improvements, passions, interests, etc. Most people even have a lofty dream. What an incredible gift that is. But, on any given day, they will not be going to the gym, not working on creating more value in some way to get paid more, not even putting in the effort at work, not sharing more time with their spouse or child, and not challenging themselves at all.

If you look objectively, you will see many people doing the opposite of what they know will get them what they want in life. I observed this as a reliable fact in myself, my friends, my employees, and random samples on social media. It is interesting to me that many strangers on social media are publishing what they want out of life. Still, their timeline of what they are actually doing is clearly the opposite of what they said they wanted. They are eating lousy food, lying down when they could be active, putting no effort in at work, spending extreme amounts of time on social media and games, engaging in destructive conflict or negligence in their relationships, etc. Worst of all, they aren't working to improve themselves. All in all, as people, we are, in fact, our own worst enemy. We hurt ourselves repeatedly when we could easily be helping ourselves. As a result, we suffer. Our overall experience, feelings, health, production, and inspiration are constantly under attack from ourselves.

Why?

Seriously why?

This is a question that I have dug very deep into for a very long time while considering my own life experience by objectively observing other people and studying different expert opinions and corresponding data related to the topic. While the experience of the problem feels complicated, the solution is simple.

Many have discussed, at great length, why people choose failure, and all have good points. But most discussions talk about the many details or symptoms of what is a relatively simple problem. We regularly hear about fear, motivation, distraction, procrastination, spiritual growth, etc. These are correct and important. I will address many of them. However, they are not the source of the solution or even the lowest-denominated source of the problem.

Sure, it feels complicated when you are living with negative results. And it is compelling for us to learn at length about our symptoms. But this is often a futile exercise. Things are getting better, and people are getting worse. Addiction and mental illness rates seem to rise as fast as our improvements to humanity. This is a measurable correlation found in many parts of society. It is the opposite of what one would expect. For example, the highest rates of increase in mental illness can be found in drug addicts and the wealthy. People with an addiction being more susceptible seems reasonable. The wealthy struggling more, however, is an incompatible idea with our culture. Money is supposed to solve all our problems, isn't it? In 2020, 21 percent of people over eighteen had a mental illness. That's one of every five people. (SAMHSA) Depression increased 52 percent between 2005-2017 for adolescents twelve to seventeen years old. (APA) We are also in the middle of the first generation to have a shorter life span than the previous ones in the U.S.

So, why?

Why don't we do the things to get what we want from life?

Because it appears easier and better to take paths of least resistance in the short term.

Our human experience gives us the psychological impressions and physical sensations that a path of least resistance is favorable, and as a result, conditions us to seek out those paths consciously and unconsciously. This is our greatest vulnerability.

But is it better or easier?

Making a poor choice most often appears to be the path of least resistance. In other words, it feels easier than accepting a challenge. Lying on the couch feels easier than taking a jog, for example. Seems easier, right? Being submissive instead of speaking your mind is easier but creates resentment. A wave from across the street instead of running over and engaging in conversation with someone you need to connect with can feel less stressful in the moment. Hitting snooze is easier than jumping out of bed. Turning on the TV after work is easier than pretty much anything else. Believing something you hear is easier than questioning it and finding the truth. And then life becomes a string of thousands of small daily choices totaling an experience of much lesser value and effect than we would like. Each choice was made almost unconsciously because it felt easier.

Even worse, these decisions compound. It isn't just that they add up; they compound upon each other. If you don't understand the power of compounding, I suggest learning it. Start with Einstein. For this purpose, understand that all your poor choices today are built on top of poor choices from yesterday. The more you have, the more you can make without replacing the previous poor decisions. And every poor decision we make injects us with a kind of mental anesthesia so we don't feel the violation of our authentic best self. That should scare the hell out of you and give you a sense of urgency.

Emanuel Acco said it best. *"The reason most people fail is that they give up what they want most for what they want now."*

This is the greatest lie we are forced to live all the time. The fundamental problem is that our most substantial sensory experiences are very limited in the sense of time. We think in the past and the future but feel sensations in the present moment. If we make our limbic system a touch more satisfied for the moment by avoiding resistance, we can feel that more than if we did something challenging to serve our future goal. We can't feel our future accomplishments and rewards until we get there, if we ever do. Our overall experience can be worsened, but we don't feel that in the moment either.

Furthermore, it is a factual lie or misrepresentation of truth. There is no evidence to suggest that most things we believe are difficult or uncomfortable actually are. Beliefs seem real but don't necessarily correlate to unmalleable facts or the correctness of experience. For example, if you ask those who are very good at self-discipline or self-motivation, most won't tell you that it's terrible and hate it every moment. They won't say it's all a miserable sacrifice to achieve the end result. That is another lie we live inside. Notice that they often enjoy it in some way. For real, they have learned or decided to genuinely derive pleasure or arousal from doing the things they should be doing, even though they are not in a state of relaxation. They enjoy the action, not only to get closer to a goal but honestly enjoy it.

Maybe these people will tell you with honesty that they love to run. It excites them to get up at 5 a.m. and crush the numbers to make a winning plan. They may look forward to finishing their small meal quickly and taking fifteen minutes to learn another language, etc. If you aren't one of those people yet, you can be.

They aren't different from you; they are doing something different than you.

Let's do a fun thought experiment to put this idea into perspective.

Imagine if we could feel a month as if it were an hour. So, in a twelve-hour day, we would feel a whole year in our experience. What would that be like if we could feel a whole year in one day? We would make vastly different choices without ever doubting them because we would be able to feel the positive results now, which normally takes considerable time. We would be intensely more intentional about our routine decisions. In an hour of your experience (a month), if you exercised for one minute, you would be in good shape after your hour. If you did it one minute per hour, you would be in incredible shape at the end of a single day.

Would you exercise for one minute an hour to be physically in good shape and increase your health and energy? Of course, you would. If you could double your income, electrify your relationships, learn a second language, write a book, and help 1,000 people stay warm and fed with a minute or two's work per hour, would you? If our perception of time were altered just a bit in our experience, that would be our reality.

Let that soak in.

If we cannot easily experience something, then we need to know how it works to believe it is working. For example, in almost all human history, we didn't know the world was orbiting the sun. Even after Nicolaus Copernicus discovered it, people didn't believe it because we can't easily experience it. If one could stand outside and feel themselves orbiting the Sun, we wouldn't have needed to learn anything to believe it works that way. That discovery was refuted strongly for a very long time. Only after people were educated on how it works with evidence and able to imagine it were they finally able to believe that the earth is orbiting the Sun. The more proof we can calculate for ourselves, the more we believe something. So, here's the no-bullshit truth of how we work fundamentally. We are all slaves in bondage by a drive to please ourselves for the moment, but we refuse to believe it's true.

We are all slaves in bondage by a drive to please ourselves for the moment.

Our egos may think each of us is the exception, but one should always ask, "What if I'm not the exception?" Look and see for yourself.

We do this even when we know for certain the long-term result is negative. Regardless of where you believe it came from, we have a built-in survival drive to avoid pain and seek pleasure that we have become far too successful at accomplishing. Pain is an indicator of injury and a signal of a potential threat of impending death from whatever is causing it. Reliably, in our ancestral past, we could survive and thrive if we could fix whatever was causing the pain. It's a decent system for self-preservation that keeps us motivated and attentive to threats to our health and wellness. Pain can directly or indirectly prohibit reproduction. Pleasure indicates health and inspires reproduction. So, over time, this drive became crucial and successful in humans, and it is strong. I believe the only reason this drive has strength is that it happens first, is quickest, and fits well in our small sense of time. Those are easy obstacles to move.

These pleasure and pain stimuli and responses get abstracted when they move around in our brains and are involved in our experiences of anxiety, procrastination, fatigue, etc. You can find most of this motivational and emotional rapid decision-making happening in a part of our brain called *The Limbic System*. This system will decide for you or make you feel like taking the easy way whenever you let it. Dr. Andrew Huberman uses the phrase "limbic friction" to describe the energy required to overcome this natural force to make the seemingly easy choice.

When looking at our primary drives, such as thirst, hunger, sex, and shelter, it is clear why they exist and persist. Without those drives, we would die and fail to reproduce. When considering secondary drives, things get more confusing. They arise from mixing our primary drives with our complicated psychology and social culture by association and conditioning, like the drive to acquire (money), intimacy, and social approval. Drives are general and broad in their abstract effect on humans. If they are successful, they persist in species. If you combine that drive with our short attention perspective of time, we have a crucial element of the problem. This part of the problem worsens as our focus gets more honed and our attention gets more attracted by better technology and a faster-paced culture.

We are getting very good at pleasing ourselves with low amounts of effort. It has become so easy to be comfortable, pleased, satiated, or aroused in every available moment in unproductive ways that we are quickly training ourselves to be hypersensitive to pain and desensitized to pleasure. It can feel like we are being chased by discomfort that is always accelerating because of our choices. We are running out of speed. It's time to turn and face it.

With this new hypersensitivity, our reality has changed to include experiencing resistance and discomfort as if they were painful. This is problematic because resistance is the only path to growth in all things. We already know this. For example, applying resistance routinely is the only way to build muscle. The only way to learn something complicated, like playing the piano, takes tremendous practice. What does it mean to practice? To practice is to develop and condition muscles, nerves, and connective tissue for proper posture, muscle memory, and coordination between your body and the new neural pathways you have been building by learning music. It isn't easy, and you can feel resistance and discomfort anytime you try to do something new or unfamiliar.

Even learning new concepts and information has a resistance that we can feel. We train for years in school on methods of how to approach that resistance and develop our understanding. Anything living must overcome resistance even to stand up. Imagine if an elephant adopted a rabbit's perspective of how much resistance it must overcome to stand. Well, the elephant would feebly lie there until it wasted away and died, unable to stand. We cannot be that elephant and survive our own progress. Avoiding discomfort and resistance makes us grow hypersensitive to them and more like the elephant who can no longer stand because it seems too difficult and painful. We must be willing to seek out resistance and discomfort to diminish our sensitivity to it.

Even breathing requires us to use our muscles and energy to draw in that breath. I'm sure you have heard the expressions, "No pain, no gain," "Anything worth doing will be difficult," "Routines and habits are the only way to success," etc. These cliches point to the knowledge that all growth and life happens through resistance of some kind. Resistance would likely become a pleasure stimulus if we felt these things in a broader sense of time. In the example of feeling a year in a day, it would be a challenge to exercise for one minute per hour and fifty-nine minutes of feeling and looking like a superhero. We would do it 100 percent of the time because the positive results would arrive close enough to the action to be felt as a positive behavioral reinforcement.

With this in mind, it is essential to notice that discomfort does not necessarily indicate danger. Discomfort and sharp pain are different sensations that can be confused in a state of hypersensitivity. They strongly correlate to different things. Discomfort is usually an indicator of growth, adaptation, or change. We may have 1,000 reasons why we aren't doing what we know we should to get what we want. But there is one common fundamental reason.

It has become extremely challenging for us not to please ourselves every moment we are able instead.

It is so tricky that we can't help it even though we know it's hurting us and holding us back from progress. This does well to explain why addicts and the wealthy's suffering rates will always go up faster even though they are typically very dissimilar from each other. They are both strongly enabled to please themselves in the moment. These people are all just as important to the world as everyone else. Anyone reading this is likely at risk of becoming some kind of addict or wealthy or both. This affects all of us in one way or another.

This isn't new information; it just may be a more source-based perspective than usual. How we hurt ourselves by irresponsibly pleasing ourselves has been discussed many times in history, religion, and spirituality. A few, for example, are the seven deadly sins, the Shaolin five hindrances, and Aristotle's twelve vices. They are all wise and accurate works, but just different ways of saying the same thing and not quite getting to the source. It's not new but is increasingly getting worse as living in the world gets easier. Ironically, we have made the world easier due to our drive to create technology and industry for progress. Before the industrial and technological revolution, life was vastly more difficult and dangerous for nearly everyone on the planet.

It's time to consider the solution. We don't want to be like the man who got shot with a poisoned arrow but refused to pull it out until he knew everything about the person who fired it. (Buddha)

So, what do we do about it, and what happens if we take better action?

There have been many answers on how to avoid hurting ourselves this way in our civilized beginnings, such as the Five Pillars, Five Yamas, and Ten Commandments. They aren't wrong. However, they are ineffective at telling us precisely what to do about it today. They're pretty good at telling us what not to do. Sure, that is still useful and relevant. But we can go further, especially in a vastly different world from when those prescriptions were communicated. The underlying truths haven't changed, but we need a fresh, actionable approach. When considering human history, there is a good argument that those prescriptions were highly effective, but only to a certain threshold. It's time to find out where to go from here, or we will perpetually revert back to that threshold.

This is the root cause of our propensity to repeat history instead of learning from it and moving forward. We repeat history constantly as cultures and individuals. We do learn from history; we don't have a new direction from here that is fundamental to our sovereign selves. Our collective past experiences can't take us forward; only our present, unknown, new ones can. We must learn something new that works.

More recently, self-help and personal progress content has become a part of our culture. Earl Nightingale talked about "the greatest secret in the world," that "every man will become what he thinks about," and he suggested you are immediately successful as soon as you "are pursuing a worthwhile goal." Even more recently, we have the book "The Secret" by Rhonda Byrne and others, bringing the concepts of laws of attraction and manifestation to the West. These concepts have paths to the solution in them, and some people find them. Inspirational/motivational speakers like Les Brown, Tony Robbins, Iyanla Vanzant, Joel Osteen, Gary V., and many others have great insight. They are all dishing out amazing perspectives and advice that can change your life. And for some, it does lead to that. But most people who are moved by these incredible speakers will not change anything in the long term. It is not from a lack of quality content. Listening to any good motivational speaker can be a riveting experience that may make you feel like you will change your life. It certainly does for me!

This is often a momentary feeling that will fade quickly as you go back to answering to your master and start pleasing yourself one small, poor choice and distraction at a time. Some motivational speakers urge their audiences to repeatedly listen to their speeches. They aren't saying this to propagate their exposure or get more revenue but rather because they understand better than anyone how difficult it is to be free from our bondage and running from apathetic attrition toward greatness.

Have you ever noticed yourself, middle-aged, or mature adults doing even worse with life than they were as young people? How is this possible? We age and learn more and more about life but can somehow get worse at it. Yes, it isn't only possible, but it's likely. The longer we live, the more poor choices and distractions we can accumulate. We dig ourselves into a deep hole when we let poor choices usurp our patterns and routines by using choice-supportive type biases to convince ourselves that we are doing something positive or justified. We can go farther down the wrong paths or get more lost. We can acquire so many chains of bondage that we can barely move or remember what it was like to be free and inspired.

How do we best break these chains?

The answer is not repression of our drives. Stopping or denying our drives has been shown to increase their prevalence in our thoughts and behavior. You do not want to pick a fight with your natural drives. You will probably lose very badly. Also, any negative force will yield negative results. Removing your drives would reduce you. Instead, we can use the energy from our drives to power us forward. But, before we can do that, we must know some things and skills we must gain. Let's start with our minds.

CHANGE YOUR MIND

Congratulations, you made it this far. Here comes the good news. We have incredible abilities that many of us don't even realize we have. We have the ability to change our patterns of thought in a deep, fundamental way that will change our experience of life. I'm not talking only about the ability to change your mind about what you want for dinner or one big idea you have. I'm focused on changing the underlying ideas, opinions, and principles that guide those decisions. I'm talking about changing how your mind works overall minute after minute all day. I mean changing the fundamental process by which we make thoughts in every waking moment and why. Changing it to have particular qualities and intentions purposefully designed to create desired results. More like changing your mode of thinking.

Thought proceeds action, and action proceeds results, so sustained intentional thinking is the first step to success. Changing when you think, how you think, and why you think is an astonishing superpower that most of us don't realize we have or aren't using in an effective way.

"Progress is impossible without change; and those who cannot change their minds cannot change anything." – Bernard Shaw.

All our results in life start with our thinking. So, when we are making thoughts randomly, we get random results directed nowhere in particular. When we are making thoughts reactively to other people, our results depend on their intentions instead of our own. When we make thoughts reacting to our emotions, we give up the authority of the direction of our results by losing our intention. When we commit to labels for ourselves, we become a prisoner of the limitations of that label's definition. Any amount of description applies an equal amount of limitation. Technically, description only works because it defines what things are not.

These are the links of our chains that shackle us to our past and present circumstances and thinking. The sum of all your thoughts in a day should move you courageously forward, into the unknown, and toward a desired result consistently and intentionally.

As you confidently traverse through the unknown, you illuminate your ignorance as the path forward. As a result, you are learning many new things at an accelerated rate. As you learn new things and have new experiences, you will gain new perspectives and more wisdom. To be able to continue doing this, it quickly becomes necessary to shed labels and change your mind about things. It becomes impossible not to change your mind when you seek the truth and gain information about where you are wrong.

I'll borrow an example from Malcolm Gladwell, 4-time bestselling author and public speaker of counterintuitive and countercultural thinking. He suggested to think of yourself 10 or 20 years ago. Notice that you have changed, and you have changed your mind about many things. You probably don't think the same styles of hair and clothing are still the best choice to represent you. Many of your preferences of food, music, hobbies, conversation, attraction, political and existential views, etc., have changed to some degree or completely. You have changed some or many of your circumstances. Most people regard the thinking of their current self as superior to their former self. I've never met anyone who would say; I wish my 12-year-old self was here to help me to think this better through. Malcolm points out that given this fact, it's illogical to believe that on "matters of opinion, we should remain absolute, especially while everything else is in motion." He suggests that we must occasionally challenge our own opinions, especially of ourselves, and "hold them lightly."

I agree that we must loosen our grasp on the feeling of permanence of who we consider ourselves to be. Our current thinking can only be our best thinking so far, and it could be our worst so far. In any case, it will change. The point I'm stressing is that we want and need it to change toward our desired result at an accelerated rate. Typically, we are slow to change, but we can speed this up. Let's make our next year have as much positive development as ten years. Malcolm and I agree that we should hold our ideas lightly and not sign up for letting them constitute our personality or who we believe ourselves to be permanently.

Really, our ideas are based on what we know now and should be allowed to change with new information and experiences. Free your identity from constraints. Malcom and others suggest finishing statements that start with "I am…" with "…for now" or "… so far". For example, "I am pro-life for now," or "I am pro-choice so far." Or start aesthetic statements with "I believe that…" such as, "Instead of saying, "That is a terrible painting." Say, I believe that is a terrible painting." All these examples and this way of thinking provide you with the opportunity to be able to change your mind should you get more information or have a new experience. So, while holding our ideas lightly and always willing to challenge them, we are perfectly positioned to think our way to positive results, letting our ideas and opinions move with us.

You have probably heard you could accomplish anything if you put your mind to it. It is true, but what does that mean exactly? Well, it means creating the conditions and ability to make thoughts toward a result constantly, no matter what is happening inside or outside of you, for however long it takes. Your actions will follow those thoughts, and you will accomplish the result at some point. But you aren't able to "put your mind to it" if you spend most of your day thinking of the bad thing that happened in the past, the thing that just offended you this morning, the thing an advertisement attracted you to, the thing that someone else thinks is important, the scary thing that might go wrong tomorrow, or whatever random thoughts you allow to appear within your attention and grab hold.

It's essential to have the skill of sustained intentional thinking. Personal progress is tremendously slow without the skill. The good news is that it is relatively easy and quick to do once you are proficient. This is an essential skill that we should all understand and practice. This skill is the key to unlocking our chains.

Yep, we are responsible for our own chains. I know we don't like to admit it, but let's go ahead and take responsibility right now. No one else is controlling what we think about unless we allow them to, and the shackles of harmful thinking that wear the heaviest, we forge for ourselves. Period. You are happening to you—end of story. If you can't accept this or don't understand it yet, that's okay. Just take a breath, stay open to it, and read on.

The victim mentality is a poison we create for ourselves, and it's real. I'm not going to get into that yet. But it is vital to hear if taking responsibility is difficult for you. And don't feel bad. It's normal to feel like you are the exception. That is an ego mechanism of some kind. You are not the exception. Stop and correct yourself if you catch yourself applying these ideas to others instead of yourself while reading. While it is true that not everything bad in your life is your fault, it's also true that you can't change anything until you take responsibility for it. The great news is that all you must do is own it, and then you possess the right to start reshaping your entire life experience. Tell yourself the truth, and you will be free and empowered.

Taking responsibility and changing your mind is best done by a trained mind. Developing the skill of meditation is how you train your mind. If you don't have experience with meditation, try this quick exercise to get a feel for it. –

Sit in a comfortable upright position. It's easier in a dimly lit place where you won't be disturbed for a few minutes if you can. Close your eyes. Start taking deep breaths in through your nose and out of your mouth. First, focus all your attention on your breath. Feel it coming in and out. Feel your chest rise and fall, your belly expand and contract. Then, give your attention to more of your body. Feel your face relax, drop your shoulders a bit as you relax, and let go of any tension you notice anywhere in your body. Don't make thoughts about these things, just feel them, and give them your attention. Don't try to describe to yourself what you are feeling; just feel it. As thoughts arise, don't fight them, don't give them attention, don't chase them, and don't try to finish them. Just notice them and let them go. Your mind will relax as you practice and stop pushing thoughts so much. As you get better at this, you will more easily slip into a state of more relaxed, thoughtless awareness. It's like an open space inside of you.

It is perfectly normal if you find it difficult to stop making thoughts and giving them your attention. In fact, the point of this practice is to strengthen the function of moving away from that grip and releasing thoughts. To help, try these tricks. Keep your breathing, move your attention to your hearing, and listen for the furthest and faintest audible thing. Or visualize a hole in your imagination that all your thoughts must come out of and focus all your attention on that hole, watching for one to pop out. Interestingly, that makes them pop out less. In time, your mind will relax its incessant thought-making precipitously. Stick to it. This will take practice, patience, and consistency. A different, more powerful experience of consciousness is the consequence of this practice.

Insight meditation allows you to mindfully observe thoughts and feelings that arise. You will be enabled to make objective decisions about them. This is truly the best first tool you need. If you can be mindful while taking responsibility for anything that needs to change in your life, it can't hurt you anymore. Before I explain more about meditation, let me lighten the mood and give you a trivial example from my youth of when I stumbled upon the method of changing my thinking to get a result.

The first time that I experienced my ability to change my mind in a very tactile way. I was sitting with my friend Ben in his cabin in the woods. It was a late fall in southern Indiana, and we were sitting close to the wood-burning stove. We were in our early twenties, sipping on liquor and philosophizing about life that we knew almost nothing about experientially. We were on the subject of perspective and somehow got the idea of changing our perspective to change our own experience. That's how we described it at the time.

After discussing it, we decided to challenge it. I noticed a bottle of gin on the table. Up to that point, I had hated gin. Just the thought of it would turn my stomach; the smell would make my mouth water; one sip of it and I would spit and gag.

So, while sitting in that drafty dim cabin by the fire, I looked at that bottle of gin and thought, *Can I change my perspective and make myself enjoy this*? Like, genuinely enjoy it. I picked up that bottle and looked it over, trying to think of how to do it, when I noticed many words on the back label. I gave it a little light from the hurricane lamp, a write-up of what it was made of. It was an eloquent, well-written piece about some of the many flavors and aromas, where they come from, etc. And how it will taste and feel as I took a sip. So, I read it a few times over and expanded on this in my imagination. For a while, I observed the thoughts and feelings that would arise. I decided to let go of the unfavorable ones toward Gin and keep the favorable or positive ones until I found, to my surprise, I wanted to have a taste.

I changed my mind. I was growing the presence of new positive thoughts about gin and the imagined experience of tasting it. I listened to Ben describe why he liked gin and empathized. I had a small drive, a little desire, to have a sip. So, I sniffed the bottle that no longer smelled like turpentine. It smelled of juniper and citrus with hints of herb. I could hardly believe it. So, I took a sip and let the flavors roll over me while holding firm to my intention to enjoy it. Sure enough, it was a pleasant experience. I was enjoying gin that, only 10 minutes before, I had detested so much that it would cause unpleasant physical reactions in my body.

As a young man in that cabin, I learned that we can decide the aim of our attention, then we create our thoughts and select which ones to keep as they arise, and those thoughts that receive our attention strongly influence our emotions. Furthermore, our thoughts and emotions affect our experience much more than I thought before. They create our experience in the immediate future with unbelievable power. Our imagination is no trivial trick; it is an incomprehensibly powerful tool that turns the screws of our relationship with reality, physiology, and matter.

I was like most people before I took my first enjoyable sip of gin. I thought that things happened to me in the reverse order. I thought I experienced things that influenced my feelings, and then I would think about them. Experience arises in the reverse sequence. We make thoughts and have feelings that arise, but with awareness, we can direct our attention internally and externally and make selections. Our selections of what thoughts and feelings to keep make deep emotions and motivate new actions. That is our experience. Then, we cycle that experience back into our thoughts. And this cycle spins on continually like a wheel getting spun by smacks of the hand of our thinking. I realized at that moment something that would stick with me forever; I am happening to me and things. They aren't happening to me. I create my experience and results. What a huge responsibility; it's no wonder we avoid it.

In the moments that followed that new experience, I thought, *Maybe I can change anything I want. I can change major things about my life.* Knowledge, communication, and expectation are the tools that power my ability to shape my thoughts. Wisdom guides my choice of what thoughts to keep cycling into my experience. As a result, I create the emotion and then experience what I want or don't want. I am always experiencing the world as I decide to, regardless of the quality or intent of my choices. In other words, I always get what I want, whether I meant to want it or not. That is, whether I am acting or thinking as if I want it.

This is also true for negative and undesirable things. If I think about failing enough, I will find a way to fail and have that experience. The failing is getting my attention, making my thoughts, influencing my actions, deciding my emotions, and defining my experience. That is acting as if I want to fail. Even if I would say that succeeding is my plan or intention, I am acting as if I want to fail.

In this example, my mind was made up that I hated gin, and as a result, my body agreed with those instructions. The action I would always take is to avoid gin. I could have forced myself to drink, which obviously wouldn't make it likely for me to be successful. But by first changing my mind, I changed the experience. So, I took the lesson and started changing my mind about useful things. I found a way to enjoy studying on some Saturday nights instead of partying with my friends. I wrote a little script in my head about the ways I would enjoy that experience, and my body took the instructions.

I remember applying this undeveloped method toward a relationship with a person I really didn't like very much, and I was able to see them in a very different light. We went from being on the verge of violence to being very friendly with each other in one day, and I didn't change a single thing about that person. I changed me. I decided my intention to connect positively with this person, took authority over my mind, and only allowed myself to make and keep thoughts that would lead to that result no matter what was said or done to me or what emotions I felt. I confronted him and told my adversary my intentions directly and honestly. Then, I showed him by genuinely listening to his complaints non-reactively while he was harsh, angry, and attempting to provoke me. I didn't comment or react to his perspective much at all. I didn't allow myself to make any thoughts contrary to my objective. I simply let those thoughts pass by and stayed relaxed. This meant I couldn't think defensively, I couldn't think critically of his argument, I couldn't think emotionally and allow his words to hurt or anger me.

I calmly listened, made it clear that I deeply understood his complaint, and suggested we put it behind us. The disagreement was already behind me the moment my intentions changed, and I had authority over my thinking. I presented him with the same opportunity to move forward into a new story with different results. After an awkward period of silence, for him, he took the opportunity, and we ended up talking about our motorcycles, which led him to invite me to his garage, where I would eventually end up working on something with him.

Practicing and using this superpower isn't difficult. If you are a person of action, don't fret; we are getting there. But first, you must ensure you have the information and disposition to excel exponentially.

Carl Jung explained how consciousness obtains its orientation to experience. "<u>Sensation</u> . . . tells you that something exists;

thinking tells you what it is; feeling tells you whether it is agreeable or not, and intuition tells you whence it comes and where it is going."(I added the underlines to that quote).

Notice that " thinking makes it so" (Shakespeare). Your orientation to experience pivots exclusively on your thinking, starting with your attention. And, by great fortune, you can change your thinking and direct your attention. You craft your experience; you always have.

Be warned, the gin experience was my first experience of intentionally changing my mind and an example, but it may not be a great idea to spend any effort learning to love alcohol. Many people reading this would probably benefit from learning to like alcohol less instead. That proved to be the case for me.

Imagine for yourself what parts of yourself you could change. Could you enjoy more genres of music? Could you get into and love a hobby that someone close to you shares, even if you detest it currently? What if you genuinely enjoyed waking up early? What if you loved dancing even if you are terrible at it? What if you were to get excited about cleaning and organizing things? What if you had fun doing things you currently pay people to do? How would things be different if you loved caring for and paying particular attention to the people close to you instead of mostly wanting something from them? What if the seemingly impossible challenges in the way of the big things you want to do became a pleasure to start working on? Keep asking yourself these questions to discover what you could change.

You may wonder why I'm focused on changing what you like, enjoy, or are interested in. You could more simply change your beliefs about things that bother you instead. It is possible to seek to reduce pain, suffering, or sadness directly in your perception. You could change your mind to experience pleasure from anything and everything, but I don't recommend it. This may seem like a good idea on the surface, but it doesn't lead to a positive result. It is risky to change your mind too far from its natural inclination. Having the power to change your mind can become a problem if you veer off its natural course too far. Our consciousness is complicated, and we don't really know how it works. So, choosing what to change and getting positive results can be difficult. It should be obvious that the right answer is most often the one we don't yet know.

I dealt with this idea for a long time before realizing that changing our minds is like cultivating nature. We want to observe and influence it in a natural direction, changing as little as possible to get the greatest yield. If we tamper with too much that we don't understand, the crop of our experience will become vulnerable.

I learned that some thinking that seems like a poor experience isn't. Instead, it's only adopting the wrong judgment about it that taints our experience. We suffer against our judgments about things, not the things themselves. It turns out that new beliefs carry as much or more baggage as old ones, and we have no experience with new ones. So, changing your beliefs is a regression back to first principles. Also, it turns out that pain is useful and fuels the sensation of pleasure by comparison. Sadness is beautiful, inspirational, and essential. Suffering doesn't just erase. That's like replacing it with absence, and absence is where new suffering grows best. Suffering must be replaced with a different meaningful choice, like a worthwhile goal or meaningful pursuit to be optimistic about. So, you wouldn't want to eliminate difficult things from your thinking or experience. Instead, you want to only influence a better direction and accept these things as a valuable part of your life.

Changing what you like and don't like, what you have a genuine interest in, and what you honestly enjoy and look forward to is the best influence on your life experience you can have. In this way, you will turn on all the power and workings of your consciousness system toward what you want without tampering with its design and functionality. Anything you have a genuine sustained interest in will get your focused attention, inspire imaginative thinking, and motivate you to apply effort and action. This is a commitment to positive change and meaningful endeavors.

So, when you start to say, "I don't like something" ask, "What if I did like it?"

Thought proceeds action, so thinking you don't like something means you won't do it, and that's the same as can't do it. You will always be right about what you decide that you don't like and consequentially can't do until you stop thinking that way. When you declare that you don't like something, you develop and sustain a negative way of thinking about it and avoid or neglect participating and engaging with it in any meaningful way. You are directing your attention and making selections of what thoughts and feelings to keep that make the presupposition remain true. So, you are functionally limiting your ability and experience. Since you are the one doing that, you are the one who can undo that.

"The improvement of a man can be measured by the level of his inner freedom. The more a person becomes free from his personality, the more freedom he has" – Leo Tolstoy.

If you decide you don't like running, you won't be motivated or inspired to run, so you will grow physically less able to run. If you don't like waking up early, you won't be as likely to do it, and it will become more difficult until you end up saying, "I can't get up early." If you don't like Gin, you'll never have the chance to develop a palate for it. If you don't like talking about your feelings, you will get very good at avoiding them and less able to share them. This logical function applies accurately and reliably to almost everything that can be experienced.

Sure, we can try to force ourselves to do things, but it's much more effective to work on changing our minds about our interest in it. You have a tremendous influence on how much you like or don't like something. Have you ever noticed that you could ask yourself a question and answer it? Are you the person who has the question or the answer? Have you noticed that when you observe an event, you can create opposing judgments about it? Are you the person who thinks it's bad, or are you the one who thinks it's good? Well, you are both. You are the person with the responsibility to select from a myriad of available thoughts, feelings, and intuitions. You are the one who decided on your interests in the first place and can deeply change your mind about them with the following method. When you do, you change the first step of the process, which determines what you are able to do and how well you will do it.

Here is a preliminary exercise to start flexing your mind-changing muscles. Imagine how it would affect the total sum results of your life if you were to change your mind about five common things. Pick three things you don't like but would be better for your intended results if you were interested in them. Pick two things you like, but it would be better for you if you didn't. Now, write them down as a statement of intention. For example: "I am going to genuinely like vegetables, reading, and listening to ideas or people that think differently than me. I am going to dislike sweets and aimless social media scrolling." The more specific you get, the easier it is. Now, pick one at a time and give it a try.

Here is a "how-to" that will get you started on practicing. It's actually more of a "how I do" that I believe will work for you too. I will take you through these skills in greater depth shortly, but there is no reason you can't start experimenting now and getting hands-on learning, even if it's through failure.

Write down, "From this moment on, I will find a way to like _______ no matter what." Now read it. Now think it. Hold on to your intention to like it firmly, no matter what you feel. Then meditate on it for a few minutes; Engage your imagination on it for a while. Let old ideas and feelings float away instead of getting your attention. Please think of the thing and imagine yourself enjoying it in different ways, be creative. Watch videos and read content from other people who enthusiastically enjoy it. Notice why they like it and try to imagine what that would feel like for you. Tell other people you will like it even if you aren't sure how yet. Finally, take some hands-on action with it while pushing yourself to find a way to enjoy it.

Hanging on to your intention and pushing yourself to innovate ways to accomplish it awakens the most effective mechanism you have. This is the mechanism that initiates your mind to reprogram the system for new conditions. If you stick with your intention long enough, you will be successful. Your success may not be what you expected, but you will be able to create or enhance genuine interest. I also use this method to sustain interest in things that are going stale by finding new ways to be excited about them. Keeping sustained interest is the most effective way to be consistent, and consistency is essential for results. Repeat this method as often necessary.

Do the opposite, but use the same practice to start disliking something.

You should have found this at least somewhat difficult; don't worry. It is probably new, and you will get better at it, especially after you develop this next skill of meditation. Changing your mind is loads easier if it is trained and you control it. During this practice, you may have felt like you were having random thoughts instead of making thoughts for a specific reason. Keep reading.

Control your mind, or it will control you.

Anyone can become possessed by their mind and answer to its random stimulus. That is where a mind is allowed to make an unbridled environment of giving attention to all thoughts. If continued constantly, a person's entire experience is consumed by unconscious reactions and following stimulated autonomic unintentional thinking. That experience diminishes our results, but it also monopolizes our attention, reducing our connectedness to our environment and body. Following random thoughts instead of directing them is like chasing after nothing and really getting somewhere!

Buddhists call this *monkey mind*. That is when your mind is aimlessly swinging from one branch to the next available branch. Our minds do not turn off on their own, ever. Not even when we sleep, left unchecked, it can cause terrible consequences. Your conscious mind is primarily a problem-solving work of art/machine. The issue is that it can use its incredible power to search for a problem even when there isn't an urgent or "real" one nearby. Hence, we can be left running around finding imaginary issues constantly. In June of 2018 Daniel T. Gilbert and many other researchers proved this with a study. He concluded:

"Another way to say this is that solving problems causes us to expand our definitions of them," he said. "When problems become rare, we count more things as problems. Our studies suggest that when the world gets better, we become harsher critics of it, and this can cause us to mistakenly conclude that it hasn't actually gotten better at all. Progress, it seems, tends to mask itself." (Harvard University. "The problem with solving problems: 'Prevalence induced concept change' causes people to redefine problems as they are reduced." (ScienceDaily. ScienceDaily, 28 June 2018. <www.sciencedaily.com/releases/2018/06/180628151752.htm>.)

"Don't be pushed by your problems. Be led by your dreams."

Ralph Waldo Emerson

We have incredibly powerful imaginations that can create positive and negative results. Take a look around and count how many real or not real "problems" you hear. If you take the physics and mathematical approach to what a problem is, it requires the given conditions to demonstrate a new fact, result, or law through inquiry. Very few "problems" you hear will adhere to that type of approach. So, they are problems of the other definition; "a matter or situation regarded as unwelcome or harmful and needing to be dealt with" (Oxford Dictionary). Those are things that <u>FEEL</u> like problems. I'm not saying they aren't real or important; however, without solid evidence of their significance to the outcome, those problems are mostly complications with feelings and perspective. Those problems will not reveal a new external fact through inquiry. It is an inquiry designed to reveal a new emotion or meet an expectation. How we feel about conditions is always a choice we are responsible for, especially when we are the ones who set the expectations and create the judgments.

It's important to make that distinction because the person experiencing the unwelcome situation chooses that perspective based on his thinking. It's a problem coming more from the inside than the outside. From my observation, most of those problems are better "dealt with" within us first before seeking to alter outside conditions. We must stop experiencing them for a moment to observe what is happening and why objectively. This is insight meditation and mindfulness.

For example, if your babysitter cancels at the last minute before work, you get stuck in traffic, your paycheck is messed up, a friend talks behind your back, etc., those are problems with a small number of possible actions and potential outcomes within your control to consider. Most of the problem for you will likely be how you feel about those things and how you deal with those feelings. Solving most of our problems happens on the inside and can take but a few seconds with practice.

For an extreme example of our sensitivity to problems, look for people saying, "I was gonna say . . . " then deliver a monologue defending against an imagined slight against them that never even happened. Think about it. They imagined a problem that didn't exist. Upon discovering it did not exist, they still decided to deliver their defensive argument and then engage in a fictitious conflict. This is evidence of our minds' incredible tenacity for discovering and answering problems even when there isn't one present. This is exacerbated by our minds' sensitivity to negative emotions. We are biologically programmed to look for threats of physical, emotional, and reputational harm to defend against. We are predisposed to be on the lookout for evil agents hiding in the brush, so to speak. This scares the hell out of me as a representation of what may be an indicator of an innate desire for conflict. It may be more like the desire to flush out hidden danger. But it is problematic when no significant threat is present, yet one is still perceived. This is much more common than one might think. You can inspect and decide for yourself. I'm suggesting where to look and how to direct your attention toward awareness of yourself.

This effect of not noticing positive progress and opportunity but instead expanding our sensitivity and finding infinite problems in wonderful situations does well to explain the discord and rise of insane ideologies in the West. The West is living in the best measurable circumstances in known history but simultaneously suffering the highest rates of negative cognitive reactions to their environment. The problem is clearly coming from the inside.

Take time to observe other people. Notice what people consider a problem for themselves and their evidence of its existence. Prepare to be astonished. Then, watch yourself do the same things. We all do it to some degree. Don't be afraid to look; getting this proof for yourself is essential for gaining experience in distinguishing between actual material problems versus emotional and psychological imitations.

Sadguru is a famous and influential figure from India who founded the Isha Foundation, which has helped over 11 million people progress through education and spiritual practices. He is a celebrated international author and speaker. He is from the East but has experience in Western culture, giving him a somewhat objective view of the West. He points out that most of our problems are our powerful intelligence working against us. He believes people suffer greatly because they have wonderful imaginations and vivid memories. He illustrates that our intelligence, imagination, and memory are so powerful that without a platform to manage them, we repeatedly relive negative things from the past and suffer. We worry about the future constantly and suffer. He believes the issue in the West is that we don't have a good platform to handle our minds. He uses and suggests yoga as the best platform. Of course, the yoga he refers to is very different from much of the yoga fitness culture we know best in the West. The yoga he is talking about is a very advanced form of meditation with movement and philosophy.

You can learn to turn off your mind by learning transmutational techniques. However, like Sadguru, I don't recommend turning off your mind completely. Stifling your incredible power isn't likely a good answer for Westerners. It is somewhat incongruent with Western culture's concepts and social structures of behaving and interacting. Like everything else, that is our natural drive; it's best to use our overdriven minds to our advantage. However, you must be able to concentrate and be mindful at your command. I'm using mindfulness here as the ability to observe your thoughts and feelings objectively as they arise and let them go or use them intentionally. It is being present and aware without reacting. The absolute best way to learn to concentrate and practice mindfulness is to meditate regularly. I cannot stress enough how important this skill is to your life. This will make everything easier and better for you, including everything in this book. It is also gratifying and simple enough for anyone to learn.

To meditate, you don't need special incense, beliefs, religious dogmas, or a particular outfit. It's **paramount that you somehow gain the skills to observe your thinking, learn to slow it down, and be able to sustainably point it in an intentional direction to do work for you**. Write that line in your notes as necessary skills, and let's talk about how to do that.

It doesn't matter how you get these skills; meditation is simply the most effective method to become powerfully aware and awake with expanded attention. Feel free to use or call it concentration exercise, self-hypnosis, prayer, yoga, or whatever you want. You can also practice turning activities into meditation, especially if they require your present attention. Playing an instrument, surfing, fishing, running, hiking, etc., are all excellent examples. However, you must do these things without letting yourself think about anything else and give all your attention to the task, how it feels, and what you perceive. That requires practice. Then, after the activity, you must put your mind to work in a specific direction of your choice. Yoga is a compelling platform because it combines meaningful activity with meditation.

Meditation is an incredible tool to slow your mind and spend some time with yourself. This is what I call creating space. One way to do this is visualization. That is where you quiet your mind and practice visualizing yourself in a room or space. Space in your mind is essential. You need space to create amazing and significant things. You need space for peace. You need space for matter to exist.

The dominant energy of the universe, recently described by

astrophysicist Lawrence Krauss, is in the space between things. The space is also where you receive seemingly magical information. It seems magical because you didn't think it up on purpose, but it pops into your head, and you do "think it" nonetheless. Another way to say it is that, sometimes, it feels like you received a message more than you figured something out. It's much like when people say, "Sleep on it," and you wake up with fantastic insight or the answer to a complicated question. You can do this while awake in a few minutes by creating mental space.

See for yourself. If you'd like more instruction on mindfulness and meditation, there are tremendous resources available. To get started, I recommend:

Mindfulness in Plain English by Henepola Gunaratana.

Zen Mind, Beginner's Mind: Informal Talks on Zen Meditation and Practice by Shunryu Suzuki.

Waking Up: A Guide to Spirituality Without Religion by Sam Harris. (There is also a great app by Sam called "waking up" that I recommend.)

The biggest thing that I do but no longer tell people about because they instantly decide that I'm crazy is I listen to my unconscious. Nonetheless, I can, and I believe anyone can. You can't think from your unconscious, or it would be conscious, of course. It's more like experiencing it than thinking from it. Also, being a detective investigating what is happening in there by inspecting evidence that is flowing out and making deductions. There is an awareness there that can be felt. With enough focus of mentally quiet attention on the feelings, thoughts, urges, memories, etc., that flow out of your unconscious, you can objectively investigate what's happening in there. When you fire up your conscious thinking again, that information becomes useful. You can get a deep, relevant, and insightful message.

Your conscious thinking is mostly limited to language-type thinking that is constrained to very few variables and is linear in nature. However, your unconscious mind can also think in images, sounds, smells, emotions, and kinesthetics (body movement). Further, the unconscious mind doesn't seem limited to space-time. You experience it when you dream. I believe our unconscious minds constantly try to help us by processing vast and highly variable information from our experiences that won't fit our limited consciousness. Once it sorts out that information, it pushes useful impressions or indicators into our awareness, such as intuition (a gut feeling), a vision or image, a desire, inspiration, a forgotten lesson, or a memory etc. I believe these are essential messages from our highly evolved system trying to serve us. However, translating it and interpreting it is no easy task. But you can listen, and you should.

Remember, the usefulness of a deep discovery doesn't depend upon where you believe the information comes from. No matter if you believe it comes from your unconscious, the universe, a god, or something else equally important. Ultimately, those are all different ways of describing the same thing as far as functionality is concerned. This is your interpretation of reality, so feel free to stick with what you know regarding belief. Again, be cautious not to over-apply belief concepts, dogma, or stigmas. More ideas and more identities are just more hurdles. I'm not saying they aren't ever useful, just not for this. Meditation is something we need, just like a glass of water. And, just like a glass of water, you don't have to fill half the glass with beliefs to drink it.

Also, your connection with your body is essential. This is much easier to experience after you have authority over your mind from practicing some insight meditation. Insight meditation, sometimes called mindfulness, focuses on your breathing to become objectively aware of the mental and physical sensations that arise inside you. It is an experience of clear awareness of exactly what is happening as it is happening. Body Awareness is an important part of insight meditation practice worth learning. And it's an enjoyable experience. I don't think I have ever done it without smiling, laughing a little, and just feeling really good. In summary, body awareness focuses all your attention on your body instead of your thoughts, emotions, and outside stimuli. It turns out that it feels terrific to be alive. You can feel it as a sensation.

Try it now. Start the same way as the previous practice and focus on your breathing. Quiet your mind. Then, shift your attention to focusing on your body one small part at a time from the top down. Feel your scalp and face and give them all your attention. Go ahead and wiggle and move them a bit to help. Feel them relax. Then move down your body, focusing on just feeling and paying attention to your eyes, lips, neck, shoulders, etc. Notice one small part at a time until you reach your toes. Then, allow yourself to feel your whole body inside and out and just stay there in that state, still breathing and not making complicated thoughts. You want to give your attention to the sensations and not to any thoughts that may arise. Let those go unfinished.

Exercise tip: With your eyes closed and in a meditative, relaxed state, put one finger into your chest. Just apply slight pressure with one fingertip. Now, focus all your attention on that sensation and hold it there. Don't describe to yourself what it feels like; just feel it. Notice how it feels on your chest and notice how it feels on your finger. As you catch your attention slipping away from that sensation, gently move it back. That means if you start to notice any other feeling or thought other than that slight pressure under your finger, let it go and refocus. When you start failing, lift your finger for a second and start over. This exercise is extremely useful for training your body attention, like training a muscle. Immediately after applying pressure, your nerves start to exhaust; with every passing moment, it becomes more challenging to feel the sensation. So, it's like a training regimen of adding more resistance. Now, try it with any and every part of your body.

I use this practice to alleviate pain and activate healing. Try it for yourself if you wish. If you have body pain, touch as near to it as you can with your fingertip and focus all your attention on your pain with the intention of letting it go or it being resolved and healed. Instead of blocking it out or resisting it, go into it fully. Keep your meditative breathing. Imagine breathing in the feeling of relief and healing. In through your lungs, down your arm, and through your finger right to the spot. Imagine breathing your pain and injury out. Up through your finger into your arm and out of your body through your breath. Like a two-way street: relief and healing in and pain and injury out. I'm not suggesting there is magic in the air; this practice uses it to heal you. I'm suggesting that there are magic-like systems inside your body that we all know are there to heal us. This is a way of instructing your mind and body that relief and healing are necessary and a priority and where it hurts.

It always amazes me that healing practices like this often get stigmatized as fanatical in some way. On the contrary, it seems obvious, logical, and empirical to me to direct your healing attention. Who else would be directing my body's systems other than me? How is asking my body to heal any different than asking it to breathe, sleep, relax, sit, or stand? I don't believe there is any conclusive evidence that healing excludes all possibility of voluntary participation.

Body awareness can recharge your energy at super speed. I'll let you discover the rest for yourself. I recommend reading Eckart Tolle's book *The Power of Now*. He is a German teacher and explains how to be present and mindful from a practical perspective. It is an easy read that is useful and palatable for almost anyone. Just know that meditation can look like whatever works for you. It needs to be a consistent practice. Twenty minutes daily is a great first goal. I suggest starting your day with meditation and another session in the evening or whenever you change gears, like getting off work.

If you are emotionally distressed or suffering right now, try meditating for five to fifteen minutes every hour for a full day. Think of it like pouring water on a big fire in your mind. It helps to keep bringing water until the fire is quiet. If you are emotionally distressed, you are reliving and re-manufacturing painful stimuli in your mind constantly. You must stop smacking that wheel of experience, or it will never stop spinning. I'm not saying whatever is bothering you is not important. But you can't do or think of anything useful under those conditions. Focus on putting out the fire for a day, then decide what to do the next morning.

FOCUS MIND POWER

Practicing meditation is step one because it is the skill of <u>Constant Intentional Awareness and Attention</u> in the present moment, actively and purposefully directing focus and attention to the present experience. It is being fully engaged and attentive to your thoughts, feelings, bodily sensations, and the surrounding environment. Once you can do that well, you can effectively focus your awareness on a single enterprise sustainably and constantly. When you can keep your mind welded to a general purpose throughout the day, no matter what is happening inside or around you, you are "putting your mind to it." You will get remarkable results.

"But don't I already have intentional awareness?" you may ask. Consider the following ideas to answer that for yourself. Intentional awareness differs from automatic, autonomic, or passive awareness, where your attention is scattered or lost in distractions, and thoughts and actions occur without conscious control. By cultivating intentional awareness, you develop the capacity to observe your inner and outer experiences without judgment or attachment. This provides you with clarity, focus, and a deeper understanding of yourself and the world.

Constant intentional awareness can be developed through mindfulness practices such as meditation, where you learn to anchor your attention on a specific focal point, such as the breath or bodily sensations as we practiced. Through regular practice, you will cultivate the ability to sustain focused attention, notice when the mind wanders, and bring it back to the present moment. The next step is to take that skill and modify it to gently bring our minds back to our specific future goal and the necessary thoughts related to it. We learn to only hang on to the thoughts that serve our intention.

Lock your mind's power on an intentional, sustained enterprise.

Let me explain this more because this is where the real art and engineering happen. Many people get control of their minds only to lose it quickly or constantly struggle to keep it under control. Minds tend to wander off constantly and are redirected by stimuli coming at them. Everyone can have a thought on purpose or create an intention. I'm talking about holding it firmly in your mind as the priority while numerous powerful attention magnets try to pull it in their direction. When you move about in real life, your attention and thoughts are always at risk of being pulled in other directions. We have a barrage of this thieving stimulus coming at us, such as notifications buzzing, advertising, body aches, painful memories, future fears, loved ones to please, bosses to satisfy, drives and desires, decisions to make, and many more.

To get an experiential perspective for yourself, try this simplified experiment: Think of the color blue and only make thoughts relevant to that. Now, go about some part of your day trying to hold only that thinking. Make a tick mark on a note card every time something tries to take your attention and thoughts away from all things blue. You may find it difficult to even be able to put the pencil down because there are so many distractions. You'll notice that you yourself are a strong distraction in many ways, and you can't escape yourself. And other people around you seem to want nothing greater than to get your attention. Try this for a bit in different places that you regularly go to get a solid awareness of the rate of distraction present in those places. That will be useful info for a later exercise.

Obviously, it's not of much use to think about the color blue. But the exercise shows you just how difficult it can be to hang on to even a simple idea without advanced training and skill. So, hanging on to a more complicated vision or goal is even more difficult. You can do it however, and when you do, it changes everything in your favor. I did this by first training my ability to be mindful or to have constant intentional awareness and attention with meditation. It is a skill like any other that I got better at every time I practiced. It's easy to learn because it eliminates most of the distractions. Then, I used that skill to practice holding a specific intention as I moved about a normal day, such as becoming a better photographer.

So, I would be doing my normal things but only letting my mind get distracted from thinking about photography-related things if they truly needed my attention. A thing only truly needs your attention when it serves a purpose for you. Just so I'm not misunderstood as promoting selfishness, things such as helping other people, the community, and the environment serve an essential purpose for you. We will get to know more about figuring out what is important in the upcoming chapter, *What You Really Want*. After giving my attention to truly important things, I would be sure to immediately push my mind back to thinking about photography by asking myself to look for how I could have captured that moment best as a picture or video. What camera, lens, angle, light, etc. What was the essence and feeling of that moment that could be felt through the eyes?

Using a mind that is trained to be ever aware and in control of its attention toward a singular mission is incredibly effective at getting results. It is even more effective than one might expect, especially while moving around through different environments and situations. For one thing, it allows you to make a tremendous number of deep connections between your intended thoughts and new novel stimuli and do it very quickly. These are the kinds of neural connections that tend to stick into your long-term memory and be useful later. It's kind of like accelerating the process we call "becoming experienced."

In different methods, the average person was measured to have between 6,000 and 80,000 thoughts per day. Dr. Fred Luskin at Stanford University has the most popular proposition that an average of 60,000 thoughts per day go through our heads, and around 90 percent are repetitive. The content of measured thoughts can average as high as 80 percent negative. It doesn't matter if these measurements are perfect; what's important to notice is we have a tremendous inclination to make thoughts every second, and they are likely to be useless to our future and harmfully negative to us in the present. Or, we can do it differently.

Try to imagine instead making tens of thousands of thoughts per day that are positive and useful for forward progress. Imagine focusing all that power on one single enterprise at a time. It's difficult even to comprehend the possibilities of this power or the quality of that experience. It is a game-changer and a life-changer. The rate of positive change and growth you can make with this skill will astound you.

This can be done for any future goal or vision, big or small. You can accomplish incredibly complex things very quickly this way, such as growing your business, becoming a better friend or parent, learning anything, changing how you feel overall, creating art, inventing something, seeking truth, etc.

You drive toward a result by being able to hold to an intention constantly.

Another familiar way to describe this is trying to stay "awakened" instead of "unconscious" (meaning a type of unawareness or distractedness). This is why most ways of getting to this state and keeping it are called a practice. Hinduism is a way of life, Buddhism is the practice of living, etc. They are all good practices. However, they inherit the same fundamental problem that has plagued us since the beginning of thought. We cannot deny ourselves of our fundamental drives without signing up for a lifelong war against ourselves.

Fighting who you are or arguing with what is are internal conflicts. You are an organism with biological tendencies and forces; that is reality. Working with that instead of against it reduces friction. Any condition or situation you don't intentionally want or need to think about but are making thoughts for anyway is an unnecessary internal conflict. Conflict causes friction, and like any good engineer, we seek to reduce friction or any kind of resistance in our machine.

Thinking is a drive. Yes, we should practice keeping it in our control and be awake and aware. But I also suggest putting it to work, just like my seven-month-old Australian shepherd. I can get her to listen to me, but five minutes of neglect and she will be back to tearing my couch to pieces. On the other hand, if I give her some exercise and tasks to complete, such as collecting ten tennis balls, she does exactly as I ask without distraction or damaging my furniture. Then she comes back for more instructions. Your mind can be trained in this same way. It can be turned into a tool of singular focus and given a job to do. That is a forward-progressing vision or goal of some kind.

Your mind isn't you, and that is extremely apparent to everyone who has disidentified from it. It is a tool for you to use. Imagine the experience of using a hammer and believing you are the hammer. Your experience would then be banging your head against hard objects. Such is the same as being possessed or fully identified with your mind.

It's not a bad idea to think of your primitive autonomous thinking like a pet dog in the respect that both will either be running wild, responding to stimulus and instinct randomly, or it will be taking orders from you on how to behave. You can experience this with yourself if you wake up and drink some coffee that stimulates your mind and start scrolling through social media or watching network news TV with no particular intention in mind. You will make thoughts regardless, they will be unbridled or run wild, and you risk being attracted to some sort of dramatics, negativity, extremism, or empty reward. Technically, every thought you make in this condition would be an assigned intention, which is volunteering your mind to be controlled by someone else, by definition.

And they will influence you toward losing awareness of your thoughts altogether. Unfortunately, our autonomic thinking drifts toward negativity. Content creators know you are more attracted to negativity and will exacerbate that effect by exploiting it to grab your attention with "clickbait" and provocative and extreme content. By the time you finish a cup of coffee, you can be possessed by harmful thinking or reacting to feelings of absolutely no utility for your life experience or future ambitions. But they will seem extremely important. The consequences of this are terrifying.

Your mind needs to be exercised with productive tasks of your intentional choosing. It also must be trained to lie down and be quiet when you say so. If you don't take control, your mind will exercise itself and create all sorts of tasks to complete. The tasks your mind will find on its own will most often be problems. It is a problem-solving machine. That's what it does. Give your mind free rein, and it will find problems. If you try, you can observe this in yourself with ease.

Take stock of your problems and evaluate them objectively. You will see that you have an uncanny ability to find problems, even if they are loosely attached to significance or reality. You may find that many problems wouldn't be part of your life if you didn't notice them or give them your precious attention. But it is often very difficult to stop giving problems attention. Training yourself to control your awareness and attention gives you the power to filter out many pseudo-problems that don't actually require your effort. The more time and energy you free up for your personal endeavor, the better. If you have children or employees, you have likely already observed obsessive pseudo-problem-seeking in other people. If you are a parent, boss, or leader of any kind, mastering the authority of your thinking will instantly make massive gains in your ability to influence others. Once you have the skill to disconnect from your internal conflicts emotionally, observe your thoughts objectively, decide to change them and hold your intention all day long, you possess authority over your mind.

Notice when you are engaging in a problem or unwelcome circumstance and ask yourself, "Is this really a problem that needs to be solved? Is the problem inside or outside of me?" Then, use insight meditation for a few minutes to observe the situation objectively. The situation will quickly become clearer, and the message that arises will be more like a useful answer or realization. Then, ask, "What is it that I wanted to be thinking about instead?"

Putting your mind to work for you also happens to be the most powerful tool for taking the perfect actions to gain everything you could want. Let's start with the fundamentals of crafting your thoughts, and then I'll give you the exercise that will change everything.

Action begins with thought. We have all heard about positivity versus negativity. This may be the most crucial rule in your thought-crafting life. What is positive versus negative? Those words and their associated ideas are convoluted and carry all sorts of weird cultural connotations. Many people will tell you that they should "stay positive" but cannot define, explain, or even give you an accurate example of what that means. We must clarify that so we can tool it for our thought crafting.

In my opinion, the act of being positive has much less to do with emotions and more to do with basic math and science. Positive and negative don't exclusively equal good and bad. What is good versus bad is a judgment. Positive and negative are more like general indicators of our perception and orientation. We typically aren't fully qualified to make judgments of good or bad because we don't yet have all the information. We don't know the outcome of the present moment yet. Even the most seemingly obviously correct judgments are impossible to quantify at some scale for lack of information. For example, almost every Westerner would agree that murder is bad. However, most of the moral landscape and successes of compassion in the West can be credited to the story of the murder of Jesus.

Maybe something can be bad and still have a positive effect, maybe not. I don't have those answers, and I'm not convinced anyone does. So, I focus on what will have a useful positive outcome for me. Spoiler alert: It turns out that cooperation, altruism, generosity, and kindness have much more utility for oneself than selfishness, manipulation, greed, or being mean.

For a more individual example, the thought, "I may get punched in the face," can be a useful thought, a prediction of the punishment you are about to receive. Suppose you have done something to provoke aggression. In that case, it is worth taking new action to avoid the attack, and it is useful to remember to avoid a similar outcome in the future. The thought of receiving an attack (a positive punishment) is different from thinking about a negative punishment where something you value is taken away. The threat of violence is adding something to your experience that may lead to a positive lesson about human aggression. With this, many future face punchings may be avoided. When the threat of violence, which is real whether we like it or not, is responded to properly, it stimulates empathy. Knowing that I am accountable for my effect on other people motivates me to deeply consider how they feel. Considering how other people feel is the practice of becoming empathetic. It doesn't mean submitting or cowering to the threat of violence is appropriate, only that it is useful to understand and appreciate the aggressor and your own responsibility deeply.

"...the hardest lesson to learn is to love your enemy." – "If you know the enemy and you know yourself, you need not fear the result of a hundred battles. If you know yourself but not the enemy, for every victory gained, you will also suffer a defeat. If you know neither the enemy nor yourself, you will succumb in every battle."- Sun Tzu, *The Art Of War*

Conversely, the thought "Everything is perfect the way it is." can be negative because it removes the possibility for improvement. If you keep thinking everything is fine and don't notice or properly appreciate that you are provoking, you may take a punch literally or proverbially. This is what we call a "hard lesson." This means a way of learning in the most difficult and painful way. The assumption is that you will learn one way or another in life. The wisdom is that teaching yourself hurts less and costs less than being taught.

In these examples, you should see the intrinsic risk of a person thinking that they are right all the time and know everything when interacting with other people. That is the way people earn regular punishment or continue to escalate conflict. No one deserves or wants that result for their life. I believe it's better to conceptualize positive thinking as making thoughts likely to have a positive future outcome instead of thoughts that only feel satisfying right now. Sometimes, it's both, but sometimes, what is positive and favorable may not necessarily seem like a pleasant or satisfying thought. If you aim to increase your positive results, then your preference shouldn't be on what feels positive exclusively at the moment. It should be on what is positively useful for you. And that yields conditions for lasting positive emotions.

One easy way to think about positivity is by putting a statement to the test. The test is *"Does it add something or take something away?"* In other words, how does it affect the sum total of what something is? For example, if you say, "I suck at meditation," you are taking something away from yourself. You are removing the vital ability of meditation from yourself. That is precisely how people will receive it and, more importantly, how your mind will receive it. This is important because your mind takes orders from you. It will make this statement into your reality. You will continue to suck at meditating. But you will be right! Who cares? You may even receive subtle sympathy if you subject others to your self-loathing complaints. Be suspicious if you feel warm feelings about being right in this self-reducing way or receive sympathy for stealing value from yourself.

The positive way to think the same thing is, "I could improve on meditation." Here, you are adding opportunity to yourself in your frame of thought. Additionally, if you share this notion, people around you and your mind will receive this as a positive affirmation for further cooperation. This is an excellent problem your mind would love to solve, and including other people will solidify your intention for yourself as well as tap into their knowledge and experience. This is a great job for your mind. You will make thoughts and then actions in that direction. Other people will be sparked with curiosity toward you when putting this frame of thinking forward and likely offer what they can to help if they can.

This is different from saying, "I'm awesome at meditating," when, in fact, you are terrible at it. That is a lie. Self-lying is a negative input toward your self-worth. This is just one example of hundreds of ways to differentiate between negative and positive.

As you start to craft your thoughts, you will learn these differences quickly and begin to notice them everywhere around you. You will likely be surprised to discover just how much negativity you have been allowing to live in your thoughts. You may be surprised to find out that you prefer negativity and behave as though you want it. Well, you do. I know that sounds crazy, but it's true.

To different degrees, people seem to attract what they want, whether they mean to want it or not. We must always work to be less attracted to negativity to get more positive results.

Psychologists have quantified that we are around twice as attracted to negativity as positivity. That is why we must work to be positive and reduce negativity in our thoughts. Our effort is required to achieve a net positive result. It will not happen without your intentional effort. Your actions all start with thoughts. When they start with negative thoughts, your actions will reduce you always. When your actions come about from positive thinking, they are an incredible growing force that serves you very well.

One important practice for this is to remember a recent thought and put it into words. Then, hold it up to the light, so to speak, and inspect it for positivity. If it's negative, see if you can rewrite it as positive. There is no reason to write down any thoughts that are simply observations or benign. So, this works better when you are dealing with something that stimulates your negative emotions. Or do a simple self-evaluation and use those thoughts. A Self-evaluation can simply be describing yourself to yourself. That is always a great place to use positivity.

At first, do this in writing. Have some note cards handy, and write down a thought or statement that you recently created. Then, inspect it to decide if it is negative or positive. Ask, does it add something or take something away from you? Does this thought point my perception in the direction I want to go? Then, try to rewrite it to be more positive. Rewrite it to add to you and point you where you want to go. In other words, more toward how you want to feel and what you want to accomplish. Craft your thoughts to point you toward your desired results.

For example, if you think, "I am too tired," your body and mind take those instructions, and you will continue making thoughts and taking actions to support that notion and reduce what you are capable of or likely to engage in. However, if you change it to, "I need to perk up" or "I want to have more energy," your mind can immediately start thinking of ways to seize that opportunity you have added and solve that problem. Your body and actions will follow suit.

Other examples: "It's too difficult" could be "This is a challenge." The new implication is that the thing can be accomplished or improved through effort. A job perfectly suited for your powerful mind. The following are examples of thoughts that can be reframed:

"I'm not good enough." to "I can get better."

"I am a failure." to "I am yet to succeed."

"I hate this." to "I could feel better about this."

"People suck" to "People could treat me better."

"Things are going wrong" to "Conditions could drastically improve."

Notice that in each example, changing from negative to positive, you are creating an opportunity to seize instead of removing or reducing what's possible. You ask your mind and body to move you toward positive outcomes instead of negative ones. In the negative statements, there is nothing you can do about them functionally or practically. It's a dead end for your mind. It's like sending a soldier an order to accept defeat and wait for good fortune or death. We don't want our situation to be hoping good fortune finds us before death. We want to create opportunities for success with every possible moment for thought. We use our trained skill of holding an intention to focus that movement toward victory.

Try to come up with or observe a negative statement and then rewrite it as positive. Then do another one. Repeat that as many times as it takes for you to be able to fire off the positive versions with ease. Like everything, the more you practice this, the more it becomes a developed skill. This practice is a great way to break negative thinking when you get sucked into it. The power of this exercise will improve your awareness and familiarity of the net charge of your thoughts. With enough practice, you will just start having a running feeling of how positive or negative you are thinking. After a while, you will notice the net charge of a thought or communication before you even fully decode it. It becomes an experience, kind of like you can taste it.

I'm to the point where I don't put much conscious thought into it. I catch myself excusing myself from situations or shutting myself down the moment useless negative discourse appears, just like I got sprayed in the face with stinky poop water. I'll even wince and groan a little involuntarily. Conversely, I catch myself getting excited and attentive toward myself and others, making positive statements. It's truly refreshing and productive. Sure, I still get sucked into negativity like everyone, but this practice has made me able to strongly combat negativity with little effort, and I believe it can for you too. To be clear and repetitive on an important distinction, I don't avoid hearing things I don't like; rather, I avoid things that don't help.

We must avoid negative thinking and negative speaking. We cannot take value away from ourselves and expect to grow more valuable.

"If you think in negative terms, you will get negative results. If you think in positive terms, you will achieve positive results." Dr Norman Vincent Peale.

"A man's life is what his thoughts make of it." Marcus Aurelius

"A man is what he thinks about all day long." Ralph Waldo Emerson

On a similar note. Stop complaining. I don't intend that to

sound crass or insulting. We all do it. It is dangerous and useless. A complaint is an expression of annoyance or displeasure. I know we are excellent at expressing ourselves. This isn't where you want to use your creative and artistic abilities to express yourself. A complaint is also an admission of apathy, submission, or forfeit. It's a way of saying that you have identified something as a problem but aren't willing to do anything about it. Les Brown pointed out that 80 percent of people don't care to hear your complaint, and the other 20 percent are glad it happened to you instead of them. You are the only one truly listening to your complaints and gain nothing positive from them.

This doesn't mean to shoulder everything. Craft a plan with opportunity instead of a complaint. A complaint and a plan are different perspectives of the same exact reality. It's a choice.

I get it though; sometimes we get shit on all day and seem to have stuff land in our lap that is too much to handle. That's okay. We all have those moments. There isn't a need to form an amazingly eloquent complaint. And you don't want to dump it on anyone, especially someone you care about. You especially don't want to create a believable victim narrative for yourself. That is deadly. Just be pissed, upset, and angry. Let it out if you can, and be just that for a bit. Then, put it down and move on.

It's healthy to tell someone about your frustration; just try not to make It a self-loathing complaint. Communicating frustration is when you vent facts that you are dissatisfied with but don't expect an external solution in return. A complaint does this but can also carry the notion that you have been wronged and deserve compensation of some kind. If outside blame is involved, it is a complaint, not a vent session. This has too much inherent risk of avoiding responsibility and forming a victim narrative for your undesirable feelings. If you cast blame, there is a victimizer, and you've de facto made yourself a victim. When you have unfavorable circumstances to vent, never forget to inspect them for culpability and responsibility. Are you the one who earned the unfavorable circumstances or put yourself in their path? Can you do anything to change them for the better? Spend your time on those questions. If it truly isn't your fault, there is nothing to learn, and you can't do anything about it, then it isn't worth thinking about anyway. It's simply another distraction. Push your mind back to your intention and move forward. "What was it I wanted to be thinking about?"

Even more important than those exceptionally shitty days, I'm talking about the regular, daily complaining. We primarily think in language, so thinking is speaking and vice versa. Make a tick mark every time you catch yourself complaining. You aren't trying to see how much of a complainer you are or aren't. You are learning to become aware of it. This alone will cause you to change your thought patterns and become much better at crafting thoughts to work for you. The awareness is your powerful tool here. It is most of the challenge. Awareness of anything eliminates its subversion. Nothing can hide in the dark when you shine a light on it. Crafting the thoughts you want is the easy part; creating the disposition to craft thoughts constantly and intentionally is the challenge.

LOVE AND STRUGGLE

Learn to love struggle and seek challenges.

Dr. Hans Selye discovered that sustained stress caused sickness and disease in the 1920's. We then made a great error and declared a hundred-year war on stress that we still haven't won because we have a flawed, narrow strategy. The mistake is to try and avoid stress. For one thing, it's not possible. Stress is everywhere; even if you massively reduce your stressful stimuli, you become more sensitive to stress. Avoiding something prevents you from adapting and learning to do it well physically and emotionally. Another flaw in the strategy is that it fails to recognize stress's supreme utility. It can make you stronger, healthier, and more performative toward improvement in the right conditions. Lastly, the most resilient, sustained, and counterproductive kind of stress would obviously be a fear of stress.

A better strategy would be to practice both being subjected voluntarily to stressful situations that have beneficial outcomes and then practicing moving to low-stress states intentionally. Don't seek to eliminate stress; instead, put it under your superintendence.

Intentionally seeking out struggles and challenges to overcome will make it possible to stay positive and motivated and point your perception in a productive direction. The way to do this and stick to it is to learn to love struggle. Like everything else that is amazingly effective, it's simple in expression. But it may sound like something you don't want to do, and your first thoughts may be that it won't work for you. That's a good indicator of how effective this will be.

It may seem counterintuitive to seek out struggle. Humans have come all this way to escape the struggles of survival, and struggling may not seem to feel good in the moment. But it isn't a counterintuitive proposition. We escaped the struggles of survival by inheriting an innately essential and dependent relationship with overcoming challenges. It is what we were born to do. Survival is in every fiber of our being, and the tools are sequenced in our DNA and present in all our biological systems. However, we have a unique and fortunate opportunity right now compared to a couple hundred years ago and before because of our success in meeting our basic survival needs. We can now choose most of our struggles because they aren't finding us every day anymore.

We no longer have to go out in the freezing cold and chop firewood to stay alive, but we can. Or we can intentionally immerse ourselves in cold air or water to activate our survival systems and strengthen our ability to deal with difficult things. The same can be said for dealing with heat accomplished with a sauna or intentionally going out into the heat. We aren't required to cook a meal from scratch, but we can choose that challenge and enjoy the struggle of the difficulty and effort required. It isn't necessary to run a mile or two to chase down a kill or deliver a message anymore, but we can choose to run anyway. We don't have to struggle to turn paint, graphite, clay, or other media into beautiful art when we can turn on a TV or open an app to see beauty, but we can choose to anyway. There is no expedient reason to learn to play an instrument when getting music in our home is a push of a button, but we still can learn one. These options are available. These options have incredibly beneficial effects with deeply meaningful experiences.

We aren't required to push ourselves to become educated about things not related to our work if we have all the answers on our smartphones. However, we can become a better thinker and more articulate by reading, listening, and discussing new and difficult things. We are connected to all the world's expert information, and it can now be sorted, improved, and communicated better than any human by artificial intelligence. So, why think or learn anything new at all? You have something unique and special inside of you that needs to be discovered, whether you believe it yet or not. The world needs that from you, and when you are going after it, you are successful and can feel it.

You gain what you need to be successful by practicing struggle and learning to overcome challenges.

The routine we want to avoid is spending our day doing things we feel are required of us, like work, housework, and personal obligations. Then, give the rest of the time to seek passive pleasure and relaxation. This situation functionally feels more like an indentured servant with downtime and superfluous rewards that trick us into staying subjugated. That routine perspective leaves us with no path for the creative development of our talents and unique contributions to the world, and it makes us feel less alive.

Instead, we want to spend our day looking at our obligations with gratitude that we have a dutiful purpose and seek to perform those tasks to the best of our ability. *"The way we do anything is the way we do everything."* Martha Beck. Then, when we want to fill our free time voluntarily engaging in a meaningful struggle, don't plop down on the couch. Pick an endeavor instead. This is your time, where you make your future and who you will become. Sure, take a physical rest when you need one, but stick to the following rule. If I need to rest my body, then I must also rest my mind. This is a great time to meditate and practice body awareness. You can recover your energy and inspiration remarkably quickly by resting with your body relaxed, eyes closed, and your mind quiet. Conversely, if you immediately surrender your attention to consuming TV, scrolling, gossiping, unhealthy food, pornography, weed, alcohol, etc.… you have effectively prostrated yourself to a master and placed its boot on your throat.

<u>Voluntarily</u> seeking challenges and struggles is the action that breaks this poisonous cycle and shocks us back to life in a vibrant way. This is why everyone should fall in love with struggling through their chosen challenges. It makes you genuinely feel better and be better in the short and long term. Emphasis on <u>voluntarily</u> seeking challenges of your choosing. And now that you are practicing controlling your thinking and holding an intention all day, you can do this successfully.

Often, people advise you to change what's required of you

instead of what you do with your free time. They say, "Do something you love" or are passionate about for your job. That indeed is best, but how? It sounds easy, in theory, to quit your job and get one that you love or start your own business endeavor. But clearly, it isn't that simple, especially if you don't know what you love. Or even if you do know, how do you become skilled enough to make a living from it? I suggest you first learn to love meaningful struggle instead of activities of passivity and spend your free time voluntarily seeking out different challenges you can accomplish.

Through this process, you become accomplished and competent while evolving your psychology and mindset toward something resembling a courageous system for achieving victories over the unknown. Be cognizant that once you accomplish a challenge, you must move on to another one. That may be difficult because it's tough to abandon something you just got good at. It would be better for your ego to do it all the time and impress people, but that isn't our goal. Instead, we want to regularly be in the struggle and the unknown that comes from doing new things that are still difficult. That is the entrance to the path of finding out what you are passionate about and developing your talents to make your unique and profound contribution to the world. That unique contribution you have inside of you is extremely valuable, and you can get paid very well for it once it's developed.

Why would we voluntarily choose to struggle? We can choose struggles we are able to overcome, which have a manageable amount of adversity. When we are successful, there are tremendous benefits that I have observed logically and empirically. Further, there is abundant scientific evidence to support and corroborate the following ideas in the literature of psychology and neuroscience.

Engaging in struggle builds resilience by improving our ability to cope with adversity and prepares us for future challenges. It also enhances personal growth by teaching us our strengths and weaknesses and exposing us to self-discovery. That process gives us better self-awareness. Choosing challenges provides us with situational opportunities to be creative and innovative. Successfully overcoming struggles will increase self-confidence and feelings of self-worth. The successes are physical evidence of ability, and you get a quantifiable sense of accomplishment. Living a life with more genuine wins earned than losses taken will reduce general stress, anxiety, and depression. Also, the process of overcoming challenges exposes us to setbacks along the way, which is a practice of dealing with small failures on the way to success. It's a practice of becoming less afraid to fail because you know how to win. It is the practice of becoming.

I first learned the tremendous value of failure from wrestling. It is an extreme example of learning to lose because when I first started, my only option was to be physically defeated by opponents in an aggressive, primitive way. I learned by being pinned to the ground repeatedly until I figured out how not to. Failing is necessary for success. There is no other way, so looking for one is useless. Walk into the fire.

Latin – Per ignem Renatus sum. - Through fire I am reborn.

On top of all those amazing reasons to be a challenge seeker who loves struggle, there is also a scientific explanation that describes how this process works at a neurobiological level (brain science).

"There is a molecule in your brain and body that, when released, tends to make you look outside yourself, pursue things outside yourself, and to crave things outside yourself." Dr, Andrew Huberman

He is talking about dopamine. This is likely not the way you are used to hearing about dopamine. Somehow, our collective cultural understanding of how dopamine works got stuck in an incomplete fifty-year-old explanation (theory). But much more has been learned in the last 50 years. We have known about dopamine since the beginning of the 20th century. George Barger and James Exwens synthesized it in 1910. Katharine Montagu found it in the brain in 1957. By 1958, we figured out it was a neurotransmitter (things that control our brains). By the year 200, we had learned much about it and how fundamentally important it is that Nobel Prizes were awarded.

Most of what we hear about dopamine comes from before the 21st century. The common explanation remains that dopamine is responsible for our feeling of pleasure when we receive a reward. While that is true to some degree, it's not the complete truth or even close to explaining the enormous role dopamine plays in every aspect of human life, especially success.

I won't give a full or overly scientific explanation here, either. However, I do want to point out some of the things we have learned over the last 25 years that I believe prove my lifelong claim that the pursuit of struggle is the most important and essential behavior for humans to engage in. Hopefully, this conversation also adds memorable context to the idea of loving struggle.

I'm going to avoid turning this into a research paper by instead paraphrasing Dr. Robert Sapolsky (neuroendocrinology researcher and author, professor of biology, neurology, neuroscience, and neurosurgery at Stanford) and Dr. Andrew Huberman (neuroscientist, podcaster, associate professor of neurobiology and ophthalmology at Stanford Medicine. Both guys are quality gateways to gaining objective knowledge in a field that is otherwise inaccessible without an extremely specific technical vocabulary and knowledge of unique nomenclature. They also cite all their sources, so seek out their work if you want a starting point for greater understanding.

Dopamine is a chemical substance that our bodies make and then release from our neurons (nerve cells); it is then picked up by other nerve cells. This signal affects movement, emotion, and the reward system of the brain. So, most of the things we need in order to be successful at anything depends on this process. Dopamine is also converted into norepinephrine and adrenalin, which is the energy that excites our body and brain functions.

Dopamine levels affect our perception of the quality of all things in life. The more you have and use, the better. It also affects the quality of an experience in our memory, like how much we enjoyed something or were successful. It is the way that we measure pleasure and success. The function of dopamine is how we know if we are doing well. It also brings energy and alertness with it! But there is a catch; increasing the dopamine effect is only possible if your dopamine levels rise compared to the immediately previous amount. So, to feel good, we must release more dopamine than we just had a minute ago, regardless of how much we had before, known as the baseline. It can't go up forever or stay up forever because the result would be not feeling good about anything, perceiving low quality of everything, and being unmotivated overall. Dopamine levels must come down. The higher the levels, the further the fall or crash. That falling is described as feeling "like shit," "unmotivated," "depressed," "uninterested," etc.

This is one reason why regular depravity is useful. It lowers your baseline of dopamine. Also, this explains why too much of a good thing is bad because it increases your baseline. If you take too much of a good thing, you will enjoy it less and less, thus needing more and more. Humans were aware of this function long before we even knew what a molecule was. A great example is the ancient Greek stoics who called for Temperance to be one of only four cardinal virtues. Temperance to them was something like moderation in thought, action, and emotion. They found it to be a practice worth 25% of all their efforts, even in a world with much fewer possible pleasures than we can access in the West today. Health professionals understand this function of dopamine and warn that it is significantly responsible for addiction. Christian type faiths understand it as the way a person comes to worship sin or a false god. All true and good warnings.

But if we focus on a positive relationship with dopamine and tool it for our purposes it becomes a way of understanding how to be inspired, motivated, curious, and successful with the caveat of enjoying most things. This is how we learn to love struggle.

Now let's look at why to love struggle through this lens. The well-known previous discovery is that our system for sustained chemical motivation requires us to have dopamine present in our brains, a challenge between us, and a reward to be motivated to overcome that challenge. It turns out that if we do have a challenge, we make more dopamine and are further motivated to overcome future challenges. The surprise is that the challenge itself is the biggest reward incentive to take on more and bigger challenges. Dopamine reward motivation is more paired with anticipation than obtainment. The brain may be wired to motivate and reward us for voluntarily engaging in struggle as opposed to finding the easiest way to a reward.

Also, how we choose to think about and judge the activities we are engaged in directly affects the dopaminergic result. Scientists can measure that using the prefrontal cortex part of your brain to think of your struggle as positive, meaningful, and victorious increases dopamine. And then your thoughts become true in your experience as a result. By stimulating certain brain functions by intentionally engaging in thought and activity that challenges us to pursue a worthwhile goal, we are biochemically receiving the highest and most sustainable reward. Obtaining the goal is not a reward in our motivation system; it is the signal to stop the motivation to some degree. Just like a racecar driver takes his foot off the gas after crossing the finish line. Our system is designed to achieve an appetitive state, not a satiated state. In other words, we are at our best and feel our best when going after a goal or reward and less so after we accomplish or get the reward.

Conversely, if we take a reward without any meaningful pursuit to get it, we don't benefit from our motivation system much at all. Even though we still enjoy the reward or pleasure to some degree, we immediately break the dopaminergic cycle that inspires growing motivation, energy, and movement. Engaging in unearned pleasure has a measurable negative impact on our overall biochemical motivation. It is removing the longest and most important stage of dopamine reward that is possible, the struggle. Imagine a 500 km race with a finish line every 1km. All winning and no racing wouldn't attract competitors or fans because it is the race we need, not the winning. This may be analogous to the significant danger of scrolling stimulating feeds on social media. It's all winning and no racing.

Learning to love struggle translates into science language as learning to engage your prefrontal cortex thinking to enjoy or appreciate the effort itself while discomfort is present. This causes a healthy level of sustainable dopamine release and fluctuation that doesn't crash. When we enjoy the struggle and think of the effort as the reward, we get dopamine and epinephrine, which is energy and biological readiness. On the contrary, if we only engage in a struggle to get to the reward after, we don't release dopamine during the activity. We will grow less interested in engaging in struggle, thereby reducing our motivation and energy to even seek a reward in the first place. These effects in either direction are foundational in our system, so the state we put ourselves in will apply to all things in our lives.

The reductive conclusion of this information is unavoidable, clear, and astounding.

1. If you choose to take unearned rewards all day without any depravity, you will be the most miserable, least motivated, and least energetic you can be in the near future. If you continue this approach, your decline will continue indefinitely until you are depressed, apathetic, addicted, and potentially suicidal.

2. If you choose to only struggle in order to get rewards and consider the struggle as terrible but necessary, you will be a bit better off than taking unearned rewards. However, you will be increasing the difficulty of staying motivated and inspired. This dramatically lowers your chances of success in anything over the long term.

3. If you choose to struggle voluntarily and enjoy and appreciate the effort it takes to do it in the present moment, you will tune up your system to be hyper-motivated, energetic, and ready for all things in life. You will constantly feel inspired, curious, and driven in all aspects of your life. Even more incredible is that you will become more and more motivated to take on bigger and more difficult challenges. This is the condition for success in all things.

When I say, "Learn to love struggle and seek challenges," I am talking about changing your mind to genuinely look forward to the struggle of overcoming challenges. A struggle or opportunity to get into one can arouse, excite, satiate, and make you feel activated to make an effort. But that doesn't mean struggle will bring you immediately pleasing joy at all times. That isn't how love works.

Functionally speaking, love is the facilitator that keeps relationships together through joy and tribulation. You want a relationship with struggle that is held together even when it doesn't feel good or requires work. Just like we love a person and are willing to have confrontations and deal with things about them and ourselves that are annoying or upsetting, we do that because we receive something we fundamentally need and have hope it will continue and improve. We believe in that union's bigger force and condition to serve a positive result. Love is the knowing we are better overall as a person in the relationship than without it. That can be your relationship with struggling through challenges. I'd say that this relationship is the best kind of self-love. It will include tribulation as well. That isn't a reason to resent struggle and destroy your love for it. That tribulation is an indicator that you are doing it right. It's also when you learn to accept your shadow self or dark side.

The concept of the "shadow self" originates from the work of Swiss psychologist Carl Jung. It refers to the unconscious and repressed aspects of an individual's personality that are often considered undesirable, unacceptable, or socially unacceptable. These are the thoughts, emotions, impulses, and traits you were told were bad. Now, you hide them in the shadows of your mind, repressing them from your expression. It can include both positive and negative qualities that we have disowned or have not integrated into our conscious self. For example, repressed creativity, assertiveness, or ambition can be part of the shadow self, just as anger, jealousy, or selfishness can be.

When we are unaware of our shadow self, we may project these hidden aspects onto others. We might attribute qualities or behaviors to others that we are unwilling to acknowledge in ourselves. Recognizing and working with our shadow self can help reduce projection and enhance self-awareness. According to Jung, the process he calls *individuation* involves integrating the conscious and unconscious aspects of our psyche, including the shadow self. It involves accepting and embracing the totality of who we are, including the aspects we have disowned or suppressed. Integration allows for a more balanced and authentic expression of our personality. Exploring and understanding the shadow self contributes to personal growth, healing, and increased self-acceptance. By acknowledging and integrating these repressed aspects, we can develop a deeper understanding of ourselves, increase self-compassion, and engage in healthier relationships.

We have been taught not to be dangerous and destructive and often don't want to admit we are capable. Then, we avoid the dark part of ourselves and any situation that would bring those abilities to the surface. Fuck that. First, it isn't true that you are docile, just in case you believe or have been convinced of that. Whoever you are, I know with certainty that you are dangerous, and it can be useful or destructive. Completing a challenge means meeting resistance that you must resolve or destroy. So, being dangerous and destructive has utility sometimes. You can activate your aggressiveness and still do no harm to others. Second, avoiding the dangerous part of yourself won't get you through the most challenging things; it will make you run from them. That is negative and reduces you. You can't afford to run. We all know we cannot cut down a sick tree with a hug. However, we also know we could chop it down like a psycho killer with a kitchen knife if we let that shadow-self off the leash. You want to fall somewhere between and have a finger on the switch.

For example, I like to exercise my body, and I usually enjoy it. But sometimes, I don't feel like working out, or I don't feel very good. In those moments the gym isn't a pleasant oasis; it is an adversary making me feel weak and think submissive thoughts. That isn't a time to be defeated. Flip the switch inside to aggressive and maybe a little angry and attack that resistance. Don't let anything you want to do make you feel weak and submissive. That's unacceptable. Sometimes, I must defeat the gym instead of enjoying it. It's the same action with the same result, and I still love it. However, I love that I was able to conquer it with my destructive side. Don't run away; never run from anything, even if it means taking a beating, so to speak. Taking a loss is a great opportunity. Don't run when taking a nasty shot of some kind; flip the switch to dark when a hug doesn't get it done.

Sometimes, in business, things aren't going to fall into place and work out nicely. That is when we must make something happen and pound out every step of the way, like hiking through mud up to our knees until we reach dry ground. This requires aggressiveness and a refusal to surrender or turn back, even though it's extremely difficult and uncomfortable. To be a person who can do this well is to be a person who can tap into their innate savagery. Sometimes, it is simply preposterous to lean over and hug the mud.

Another example is when someone attacks me; I like to defeat them with listening, inclusion, and genuine consideration. Usually, that's enough to dominate or cooperate. That is a show of strength by the non-defensive reaction. It is not the same as giving in. You don't have to give any ground to listen. But, sometimes, it doesn't work; they cross a line, and I will confront them. If I must defend myself and fight, so be it.

I hurt some people when I was young and angry, and as a result, I was afraid of my shadow self for a long time. Through my own experience of running from it for so long, I could see how damaging it was to deny that part of me. I have since accepted that part of myself and use it with caution and control. It's okay to look into your darkness, see how dangerous you are, and call up some of that energy to destroy whatever weakness is in your way. If anything, including you, gets in your way and won't move, get angry, get mean, and get through. Notice that we are destroying our own weaknesses, not destroying things or people.

Latin from Virgil's *Aeneid*: "*Flectere si nequeo superos, Acheronta movebo*" –

If I cannot bend the will of Heaven, I shall move Hell.

Keep yourself rooted in caution and control to make sure you are acting honorably, especially toward other people. If you need to confront someone or defeat them in some kind of competition, attack your weakness, self-doubt, and fear of failing with your aggressiveness. Attacking another person or acting dishonorably won't bring personal success; instead, it will harm the best parts of you. If you are going to win a competition, it means the most when you allow the other person to be at their best with all their advantages and are victorious anyway. You conjure up your dark energy by refusing to accept defeat or quit. When neither meekness nor avoidance are acceptable options for you, assertiveness and aggression become your only options. You are voluntarily backing yourself into a corner. You will be amazed at what you are capable of.

If your struggle experience turns into sustained misery, that indicates that the particular struggle you selected isn't appropriate or timely. Withdraw and regroup. That isn't the same as quitting or running. Notice that we are learning to love the struggle first, not the challenge. Struggle isn't intense pain or suffering. It should be a task that requires an accomplishable amount of effort that will last a reasonable amount of time.

Loving struggle isn't impossible or even unlikely. In fact, you will find that it is a more natural relationship than you may have with trying to please yourself in every fleeting moment. Struggle is what you were born for. Another way of saying it is that victory is what you were born for. There is no victory without struggle.

We have evolved in every way to successfully struggle through challenges, solve problems, and create solutions our entire lives. Without struggle, it is very difficult for us to possess meaning. And as a result, having a meaningful pursuit is when we are the most alive. Seeking out meaningful pursuits that are challenging activates dormant genes in your epigenetic code. Epigenetics is your behaviors and environment causing changes that affect the way your genes work. It doesn't change your DNA but decides how to read it to accomplish what you are asking of your body and mind. These are lasting biological changes you get to keep after the struggle has ended. Struggling through challenges also stimulates neurogenesis, the creation of useful new connections in your brain. You are more alive in this state, and you can feel it. It is what you were meant for.

It's not necessary to be an expert in science. However, it's very useful to know that the science reliably shows that it doesn't make much difference what challenges you are choosing to voluntarily struggle through, only that you are doing it as far as stimulating your system is concerned. The moment you start to struggle with the intention to overcome a challenge, your body and mind start physically changing to be better at doing just that. These are changes that serve your goal of being able to achieve success in anything. You can feel these changes, and they will carry their power with you into all parts of your life.

So, it can be supremely useful to do seemingly unproductive things such as crossword puzzles, playing chess, practicing standing on your head or balancing on one foot at yoga because it's changing you to be better equipped for the things that matter to you later. Of course, it's also most useful to pick things that are important to you, that you are afraid of, or that are new to you. Then, just start doing them. Do them poorly, but use your new skill of holding your intention to do it well.

I'll get into this later, but it's worth mentioning here that this pursuit of meaningful struggle will often cause the side effect called happiness. I believe that happiness is not a sustainable state of being; it is best described as a positive and wonderful side effect of meaningful living. In my opinion, there is no good evidence that it should be a continual state of being, and that may be a terrible misunderstanding that plagues, confuses, and frustrates humans endlessly because it's like looking for a beautiful sunset all hours of the day. It's the wrong expectation. All day, you will be miserable and squinting in pain in a blazing sun, and at night, you will be miserably cold, bored, and depressed with so much focus on the absence. Then, the sunset you finally witness will certainly be anticlimactic and not worth the unproductive effort. There is a kind of necessary cycle of differentiating experiences that are required to make happiness possible to feel properly. I think it is a mistake to grasp onto it and try to make it permanent. However, as you have probably noticed, a day full of meaningful interaction, engagement, and work that ends in catching a sunset will stop you in your tracks and take your breath away. Especially if you can quiet your mind.

I remember one distinct way I observed the power of struggle for myself and other people. I have been an entrepreneur and business owner for fifteen years. I have developed and operated many types of businesses with employees. One big focus is constantly learning to unlock the incredible potential of employees to do amazing things. I have always believed that if I can make my people successful in a business, I will be successful, and the company will profit. And I've always found that to be true. However, making employees successful and happy was more complicated than it appeared.

I went above and beyond in one business to create the best work environment imaginable. I made it possible for the staff to have everything they thought would make them successful and happy. They made 30 to 50 percent more income than the industry average and were allowed to work 30 to 50 percent less. They could choose to make double everyone else or work half as often. We also approved all time off with no limits, provided free education, and created a system to provide everything for them, so all they had to do was focus on their craft at work and not be bothered with other types of requirements or stress stimuli. We made the employee-tailored perfect job for them.

It was a catastrophic failure. In a relatively short time, everyone was miserable, complaining, fighting, underperforming, creating imaginary problems that couldn't be solved, etc. Finally, almost all of them quit in a strange type of mutiny. Nearly every one of them blamed the business for their blight. It was the strangest thing I have ever seen unfold in business, and I wanted to learn how that could have happened. I ruled out a gas leak or a mass Kool-Aid poisoning that may have caused delusions. Then, I discovered the problem. They had no struggle, no challenges, and an abundance of idle time and thought energy without a way to use it. As a result, they had no victories, no accomplishments, no measure of self-worth, and no outlet for their drive to solve problems. So, they created problems and struggles. They made unhealthy, unreasonable, and unproductive struggles that led to abstract conflicts. Many were genuinely suffering in an environment that provided everything we believe makes us successful and happy. We were wrong. They were prisoners of utopia.

Conversely, military people most often describe an extensive training camp or even a combat tour as the best part of their lives. How could deprivation of essential living elements while under all kinds of physical and mental attacks be good in any way? How could the most brutal example of struggle be the best time of one's life? Well, I'm sure there are several reasons I can't understand. But there are some I can. My grandfathers and both of my parents served, and both my siblings fought different wars in the Middle East. Many of my wrestling comrades did tours, and some made enormous sacrifices. I am no stranger to military culture, even though I didn't serve.

The soldiers who live to talk about it are winners to some degree, as they are still alive. Soldiers are forced to face a constant barrage of inescapable struggles to overcome challenges. Every day, they are accomplishing and overcoming. Furthermore, they have no choice but to struggle alongside other people in their company and are rewarded with the deepest kind of camaraderie, confidence, self-reliance, self-worth, and more. Also, they are lucky enough to experience deep contrast. Contrast is what resets our sensitivity to pleasure. If you want to know how to turn a simple, warm, safe bed or a loving hug into the most extraordinary and cathartic experience of your life, ask a veteran of war.

From my experience, I feel the most alive after honorably winning a fight, second most alive after honorably losing a fight, and the least alive by not fighting at all. It always turns out to be myself that I am fighting.

These are extreme examples that I'm using to illustrate how

wrong we are about what we think we want. Recall earlier when I told you it was a lie we live in. We are so wrong about what we believe makes us happy and successful. We are wrong about how we fundamentally work. Fortunately, how we do work isn't difficult to figure out.

Gaining new material things becomes less necessary for pleasure. This is such a rewarding and fun trick. Try to imagine feeling the extreme profundity in what we call our ordinary lives. That is what contrast and mindfulness can give us. If you want a significant stimulus to experience this, go camping alone in the woods or desert with only the minimum supplies. In just a day or two, it will start to set in. You will be amazed or reminded of how much pleasure you can derive from things you have been desensitized to. You will start having wet dreams about orange juice, climate control, or a shower. You will notice how much your friends and family mean to you. It's a good idea to do this once a year if possible.

Let's get down to the major "how-to" platform I use. I suggest starting your training with physical exercise. Physical exercise has an obvious struggle we can easily identify, and we can practice learning to love it. Most importantly, it has easily observable results. Furthermore, we are 100 percent certain it will benefit us to the highest degree. Finally, exercise is routine and gives us a great platform to practice our mind training and self-engineering. I know we have all heard the benefits of exercise a million times, and for good reason. One reason that isn't mentioned very often is that your mind and thoughts are a product of your brain, and your brain is a body part. So, exercise improves and strengthens your mind. Our bodies are not separate from us. We are not a person in a body. A powerful and efficient body overall will increase and compound your ability to make improvements in yourself and the world.

Also, the self-confidence gained from regular exercise is something everyone deserves and drastically empowers us to make moves we may otherwise be timid of. It's important to say it this way: Our emotions come directly from our bodies. Improving your body directly enhances how you feel. It is a unidirectional causal relationship. We often mistake this relationship between our emotions and body as a bidirectional causality. That is when you think that there are two things causing you to feel bad. The confusion is that we can often "feel bad" and believe there is some mental stimulus or circumstance that needs altering to feel better. That may be the case if your body is healthy. But, if your body feels bad, your mind will feel bad regardless of the other changes.

You will use this template repeatedly while you journey to your most amazing life experience. We are inputting physical exercise here, but any struggle that aims to conquer a challenge and ultimately accomplishes a goal can be used. You will appreciate this next part differently if you already have exercise and fitness mastered. Feel free to read it as an experienced champ and then input something different. Such as learning how to do something new, becoming better at your job, improving, finding a relationship, being a better parent, or anything that sounds attractive but difficult. You can do it.

Put your mind to work first and set a destination (goal).

First, create a preliminary schedule designating the times in which you can do the activity. I suggest keeping it to one hour daily, five days a week. Don't let yourself make distracting thoughts about this proposition yet. Just find or make a one-hour block in your schedule five days in a row and claim it for you. Imagine that hour is a hill and stick a flag in it while screaming, "This is mine!"

Go ahead and set that alarm, but instead of hitting the gym when you wake up, start thinking. Start with a few minutes of concentration or meditation and clear your mind of noise. Tell yourself, "I am going to love this struggle." Make the thoughts, turn them into words, say them, and listen to them. Write them down if you can't focus well. Then concentrate on imagining yourself in great physical shape, enjoying the hell out of some type of strenuous exercise. Don't be ashamed. For example, imagine yourself ripping out some squats with a heavy load. Or mountain biking up a steep hill with each push. Or, if you are starting from a poor physical condition, envision walking thirty minutes outside with your heart beating in your ears and your chest burning a little.

I want you to really get into this small vision. Let yourself feel the burning in your legs and the pressure in your head as if you have been thirsting for it your whole life. In your vision, you are the creator of everything. Be as strong as you like, and that burning feels terrific and pleasurable. Complete just a few minutes of this, and then open your eyes and turn your mind loose on gathering data for the new instructions you just gave it. You just set your destination and will revisit it often until you reach it.

This next part is easy but a dangerous risk of distraction. If you have a smartphone and internet, subscribe to some fitness channels, websites, and apps and read articles on the topic. Search videos on fun and exciting exercises or something you have always wanted to do. Look up some upcoming fitness events a few months out that you can do. Fill your head with all the think food your mind will need. Follow your desires and put them to work. Look for activity ideas and exercises that you are already attracted to. Don't click on any other stuff on your phone. It all can wait; you are usually asleep right now, anyway. Your hour will be over soon, and you are finally doing something for yourself to change the game. Don't get distracted. If you know you can't handle it, leave that phone on the nightstand and do it the old-fashioned way. Magazines and books still exist. In the last few minutes of your hour, close your eyes again and fantasize about being excellent at some physical activity. Focus on making yourself appreciate the struggle. Try to imagine the sensations as you do and let yourself feel them as a positive emotion.

Open your eyes. Now, you are going back to everyday life, but changes have been made, and your mind machine is turning and rewiring in the background. It has already started affecting your body systems: central nervous system, endocrine system, etc. If you focus, you can probably feel it already. To keep gaining momentum for this week, you will want to make regular thoughts about exercise and activity throughout the day. You must keep feeding this wolf that you just conceived inside you, or it will die. This will require you to be aware of your own thinking and be able to redirect it. Recall what I previously said about meditation and concentrating skills. Most people I meet don't have this ability or have lost it. It is a skill that will atrophy if not used. This is an essential skill to practice. You want to be good at this, or you are lost at sea all day long, going nowhere except down your to-do list. This is where things get different. Most of the time, we knock something off our schedule, move on to the next thing, and forget about the last one. This time, we are going to hold our desired thoughts in our minds like a film on pause.

Throughout the day, think about these chosen thoughts. When you have this mastered, you are officially at the helm and in control of your life. At first, holding your destination, or thought construct, isn't something you can trust yourself to remember consistently without help. Your ego will quickly fool you into forgetting ever reading this and will start thinking about some ridiculous imaginary fear or real-life drama. So, use what you have around you. Tools, you have amazing tools. Set the alarm on your phone for every hour on the hour, for example. Make it a silent alarm or tell people it's a medication alarm. That is the truth, after all. On that alarm, take sixty seconds and a couple of deep breaths, take a big drink of water, clear your mind, and remember what you wanted to think about. It's okay if you don't have time to indulge in any more thoughts at this moment. Sometimes you will; sometimes you won't. But you will now have the chance to be in control. This method reaches much further at changing you than just the subject at hand. I will get to that in the following couple of chapters.

At some point during this week of activating your mind, you will start feeling excited to get started at exercising or whatever struggle you have chosen. Feel free to start early if you are excited about getting to the struggle. But there is more to know before taking the best primary action. I just gave you an outline and exercise to get you started. You don't have to be an expert to get started. Now, we will dig into what is happening here and the many explicit things you can do to make fundamental, lasting change for the better.

WHAT YOU REALLY WANT

We all want to get somewhere better than where we are. And, when we take action and embark on that journey, we are doing what we were born for. At that moment of decisive action, we are doing what makes us the most alive and, ultimately, the most satisfied. Just like in this moment for you right now. Notice it's the journey itself that we need. It isn't the destination. There is no end destination to arrive at. There is no end destination to anything in the universe; there has never been. You don't want an end destination. Arriving at the end of your potential and possibility while you are alive and able would be absolutely abysmal. The only final resting place that may exist is your deathbed.

There are many amazing destinations on this journey; they simply aren't the final destination. They are waypoints, or better vantage points, to see where to go next. That is something to be grateful for. Never being able to get to the end may seem a depressing notion. That is simply a misunderstanding, and we often don't interact with this destiny correctly. Once you let this truth become the frame of your perspective and start living in it mentally, everything will feel more natural. You will always be satisfied with where you are in life once you fully appreciate that there is no arrival but rather perpetual motion. You don't want to permanently arrive. That is the same as quitting, and it can feel like you're dying or not living.

You should have goals and direction. You need to have your next destination in mind. You must always know it won't be your last, but you will have a chance to reap the rewards.

If you were the captain of a treasure-hunting sea vessel a thousand years ago, your best approach would parallel a good life approach. You are a treasure-hunting vessel, after all. You would need to map out places where you think you might find treasures. You will have to map out the best navigable path to get there. The wind won't blow you straight there, so you will be correcting course constantly. Along the way, you will encounter other lands, islands, shipwrecks, people, etc. All of these things can be ripe with attraction or treasure and danger of their own.

New prospects may even inform you that there could be a more worthwhile destination you hadn't known about before. So, you will have to decide several times whether to stay on your path or to make a new one. You must decide what to be distracted by and what to let go of. The more you stay on course to a particular destination, the quicker you will arrive. How do you know if your original destination is better than the new possibilities you have discovered? The answer is that you must truly know what you want next.

If you don't truly know what you want, you won't be able to stay on any course very long and will get caught in a perpetual pattern of changing paths and never finding treasure. What is a treasure to you? What do you value most? These questions aren't as easy to answer as you may think. There is a real epidemic, especially in the West, of people being caught in a futile exercise of searching for and obtaining things they believe will make them happy and fulfilled, resulting in further misery and disappointment.

Before we get to figuring out what you truly want, let's say you make it to a destination. This is a perfect time to reap the rewards. This is when you stop for a bit, rest, and dig deep into your gratitude. If you know that you will embark on a new journey soon, you have the freedom to enjoy yourself. Knowing that you are taking a temporary respite from progress or growth keeps pleasurable activity in the realm of earned and necessary reward instead of hedonic excess. Take the time to repair your body, mind, and ship, so to speak. You can re-familiarize yourself with completely guilt-free relaxation because you have plans to go at it again soon and set sail. This is a perfect time to feed your soul or greater purpose and contribute to the community. Take some time to flex your empathy, be charitable, and share your new knowledge and wealth to make a better world. You will, after all, have more treasures to reap from a more prosperous world.

This doesn't mean you can't hold down a steady job, take care of the same home for sixty years, raise children, or do anything that requires this kind of discipline and follow through. The reality is the contrary. These ways of living in themselves have loads of adventure and hidden treasures to uncover. You could choose to go after proficiency in work skills that are not required of you. No one is stopping you from picking difficult and interesting things to teach your family that you first must learn yourself. Decide to DIY at least one house project a year that pushes you into unknown territory. Decide to learn and practice becoming a driving force of great relationships in your family. Have a personal creative endeavor that you can give attention to in those moments when obligations are met.

I still remember the look of disbelief and inspiration on the faces of my wife and daughters when I presented them with a damn impressive realism sketch that I made from a portrait of my youngest. I couldn't make a proper stick figure a few months prior, and almost no one could read my handwriting. My youngest daughter brought my lack of skill to my attention by jesting that at seven years old she was already a better artist than me. My feelings weren't hurt, but it occurred to me that drawing was important to her, and I had a chance to find a treasure. So, whenever I would get a few minutes in the evening, I would practice sketching. I was terrible at first, of course, but eventually became skilled enough to produce a decent work of art. The treasure for me wasn't that they all were very impressed and adorning; it was that they were all inspired by my ability to change and improve. All of them instantly made their own plans to improve on something and work more on a creative endeavor, and my youngest immediately ran to gather her art supplies.

Becoming hungry for your treasure is the way to hold together stable obligations and responsibilities without becoming stagnant and miserable. Being a treasure hunter with a home base can empower you further. This is how you realize you can't wait until retirement or an empty nest to start living. This is how you prevent destroying yourself, your family, your friends, and your environment with resentment.

The conditions you need to create are available and necessary right now. You simply must figure out what your next treasure is. It can be traveling, learning, or being educated on a particular interest. Go after a creative, artistic, or cultural passion. Start training for a specific activity or event. Make a plan to electrify your relationships with people you love. Start looking for new people to love and new relationships. There are millions of treasures out there to choose from. What's important is that it must be for you and what you truly want. How do you figure out what you truly want?

The process I've laid out so far is the best path to finding out what you truly want and don't want. So far, we have learned how to:

Accept and embrace ignorance, which opens the door to what's possible. Control the mind and become constantly aware to create space for growth.

1. Change the mind and focus it toward success one singular enterprise at a time with sustained intentional awareness.
2. Voluntarily seek new challenges and love the struggle to improve the ability to improve.

Thus far, you have learned to put yourself in a position of self-control that is pointed toward self-mastery. *Vincit qui se vincit* – One conquers, who conquers oneself. You should quickly start becoming able to let go of things inside that were clouding your current most valuable purpose. Your most valuable purpose is what you truly want, and you can tell when you come across it by how it feels. The practices in *We Aren't Who We Are* will bring this inspiration into the light, so to speak. If you put forth an honorable effort, the likelihood that you will be struck with deep inspiration in the near future will increase dramatically. I believe it is a certainty. It will strike you as the most meaningful and important endeavor at the moment, even if you don't know why. Especially if other people may think it's stupid or inappropriate. When you notice that inspired feeling, don't apply reason or question it yet; you must foster it and give it attention, or it will fade quickly and can die. You are looking for that curious thread to pull on. And to have the energy and time to pull on it and chase your inspiration. To do so, you'll have to let go of some things outside of you.

Sometimes, serving yourself and your purpose instead of someone else is difficult. This is especially true about raising children. You are entirely responsible for providing for and taking care of them. However, the truth is that they will be influenced the most and learn the most from what you do, not what you say. The best way to raise a child to be excellent is to be excellent. The best way to raise children to be miserable, resentful, and self-destructive is to be those things in front of them. And, even worse, make them feel responsible for your misery because you sacrificed yourself for them. If you want your kids, spouse, friends, and employees to be inspired to light the world on fire, show them how it's done. And include them when you can, especially with the difficult things.

Another thing we need to get out of the way before we can determine what we really want is our irresponsible pursuit of power. I mean irresponsible in the strictest sense of its definition. That is a pursuit of power without accepting responsibility for it. Understand that if you seek to control anything and succeed, you are entirely responsible for it. Whatever degree of control you have over someone always equals the degree of responsibility you have for them as well.

For example, if you adopt a puppy, you train it well and understand that both its good and bad behavior are your doing. Or you train it poorly and must know that its behavior is also of your doing. Otherwise, you will spend ten to twenty years desperately yelling at a confused dog for doing exactly as you trained it to do. That is irresponsible power of control. It is that way for anything you put under your control.

We can apply the same logic to a spouse, boyfriend, girlfriend, platonic friend, or colleague. If you are focusing on what you want from them or to get them to fit into your idea of what they should be and do for your purpose, you are likely adjusting your interactions with them to serve your agenda to some degree. You are also adjusting your presentation to them to control what they think of you. You are seizing control of that relationship instead of letting it flourish naturally and having faith that it will. Unfortunately, this circumstance diminishes what people can bring to you in the relationship. It's like the best they can do is deliver something short of your expectations, and you never get the blessing of them surprising you with their unique contributions.

To seize that subtle control of a relationship, you are likely drawing that person closer in proximity, such as making thoughts and taking action to sit where they sit, talking where they talk, being in their inbox and soliciting them to your inbox, etc. You will catch yourself doing and saying things to make them agree with your opinions and ideas. This is not the same as seeking acceptance. It's like attempting to make them an extension of you or a mindless soldier in the gang you lead. You will find that after some time, you are only left with people you were able to persuade to give you some level of control over them.

Sure, you probably don't seek control to the extreme levels of a tyrannical leader. Still, even the smallest amount of behavior in that direction or of that type is catastrophic to available energy and time to spend on controlling yourself. Behaving this way at all requires all your attention. So, even if you only seek to apply 1 percent control over someone, it requires 100 percent of your attention for some measure of time. You should understand just how precious and important your attention is to your success by now. It is the only fundamental resource for intention. Besides, letting go of control isn't a risk; people don't disappear or lose interest in you because you let them go free. On the contrary, people will generally find you more interesting and will volunteer to sit with you and message you under their own independent cognizance. They will seek your acceptance and bring you their greatest gifts of unique ideas, feelings, experiences, and behaviors, especially if you listen to understand them deeply.

Nothing you could ever say will attract a person as effectively as listening to them.

We must let go of any motivation to control others who aren't our children. And I only seek to control my children only when absolutely necessary for their development and physical safety. They also need to learn to become who they are independently instead of who I imagine them to be.

With the weighty load of responsibility in mind, how much control do you really want over your spouse, friends, children, colleagues, neighbors, strangers, even? How many material things do you want to have to take care of and carry physically and mentally on your journey? If you make the heroic choice to take 100 percent responsibility for yourself, how much else can you really lift? More importantly, is it even a good thing to control anything or anyone other than yourself? Is having authority over yourself enough to accomplish everything you sought to do by controlling everything outside of you in the first place?

An excellent way to think of this is to focus on your influence instead of control. Great people influence a great number of people and are celebrated. Tyrannical people control many people and are annihilated, usually by those under their control.

Sic semper tyrannis – thus always to tyrants.

This is important because a strong network and powerful influence of clients, employees, colleagues, etc., are important tools for becoming successful, but we must be cautious not to seek control. Wielding powerful influence instead of wielding controlling power is not a lesser or weaker position. It's a subtle but significant difference. With influence, you are seeking to have the <u>capacity</u> to affect the character development, behavior of someone or something, or even the effect itself. But you are not taking as much responsibility as when seeking control. You are instead trusting and arming that person to perform well and be responsible for themselves. You have faith that the thing you influence with strength, honesty, and righteousness will serve its perfect function, even if it isn't what you expected. That differs from the power of control, which requires you to have the ability to direct someone or something. That is to manage or govern.

I have raised two daughters and had two marriages. I have employed thousands of people in many types of businesses. I have possessed many material things, hobbies, instruments, and tools. I have adopted far too many damn pets in my life. I can tell you with cheeky certainty that managing and governing things other than myself is exhausting and counterproductive. Most importantly, you won't have the proper energy and attention to spend on yourself if you overdo it. As you decline in energy, attitude, and effectiveness, so does the quality of your external control. The result is a shrinking existence, chaos, and suffering. You will be responsible for the suffering of those you seek to protect or nurture if you have them under your control while you regress.

On the other hand, I have also learned that wielding powerful influence by always starting with governing oneself is replenishing, empowering, expansive, sustainable, and truly effective. This path gets things out of the way and will clear up what you want. We always discover that we don't actually want to control everything but instead want it to all go in our favor. We want our environment to be friendly to our cause. Ironically, it already is. That fact becomes apparent after we accomplish a shift in attitude.

Here is a suggestion on how to force this change. Start with you. Sit alone in the quiet with something to write on. Take some deep breaths and clear your mind of chatter. Let go of the recent past and upcoming future just for a bit. Take a long, honest look at yourself at this moment. How do you feel? Take stock of one thing you could do for yourself today and two more things over the next month that may require planning. Be cautious not just to please yourself expediently or temporarily. Ponder, "Will this help me be better or just feel better?" Sometimes it's both. Sometimes, it's not, and the things you need to do to care for yourself aren't immediately pleasing at all. Make the distinction, and then make these two short lists. Just pick a couple of high priority. It doesn't matter if they are the best choices, and the list won't be complete; just make a decision.

Do for myself today 1._________________________

Do for myself this month 1.______________________

2.______________________

That was painless and important. You care about yourself, and you are the only one you can count on completely to take care of you. Commit to doing these things. Keep your commitment no matter what.

The next thing on the list may not be painless. Write down one thing you need to change about yourself that you can start doing immediately. Tell yourself the truth here. Trust in your strength. You are stronger than you may think. Every one of the thousands of people I have met is stronger than they think, including me.

Thing I need to change

____

_

Something I can do about it today

____

—

The last thing on this list will give you the time and energy to accomplish these things. It will also be the platform for your change from control to influence. Write down at least one person to relinquish your attempt to control them. Someone to release from your grasp and responsibility. You don't need to separate in proximity; just let go of control. If you honestly can find any desire to control anyone inside of you, even on occasion, great! Skip this step. But first, look very closely and honestly at your relationships; uncovering this behavior in yourself will take some effort.

Person to release from my control

—

Reevaluate and complete this list every day for a while.

Now, write down a couple of specific ways you could positively influence the person instead of controlling them. One of the best ways is to ask them questions about things that are important to them and actively listen without adding anything. Just accept what they have to say about it. Be genuinely enthusiastic about anything they present to you. That is anything they come up to you and say or show you. Respond enthusiastically if they make a proposition of some kind. You don't have to agree with it, but you also don't have to disagree. Trying to understand instead of trying to be right yields influence. Randomly, do something nice for them after you have done the thing for yourself. Please create your own ways to positively influence or encourage the person that allows them to surprise you. Have faith and trust them.

However, make sure you are also honest with them if they betray your trust. Even the best people will do this occasionally; everyone makes mistakes in relationships. Go headfirst into a calm verbal confrontation when they do or say something mean or intend to diminish you. You cannot allow that. They won't be happy about it at first if it's new, and that's okay. Their perspective of you will quickly change toward a place of greater respect and affinity. You will be surprised how fast this type of relationship improves when you have clear boundaries. Yes, it's possible they can't handle it and will leave you or retaliate in some way. That's much less likely than you think, but it is also okay if they do. Most likely, they will return to you with a better disposition and higher opinion of you if you can stand your ground behind a fair line in the sand. If they don't return, you have influenced the best possible result for your life because you have eliminated an unreasonable force of diminishment.

Make sure you are calm and aware enough to choose your words carefully toward the desired result of improving how you are being treated. Go ahead and say exactly what you think is true and attack the behavior, not the person. For example, "I believe you are being mean, I don't like it, and I won't accept being treated this way." Then make your exit. That is very different from calling someone a dick head and then trying to convince them that they are a real prick and hanging around for their counterattack on you. That's a fight, and you attacked the person, not the behavior. You could instead throw some positivity on the confrontation by saying, "I value you and our relationship, and I believe we can do it better than this." That is the kind of confrontation I am talking about.

Safety disclaimer: I don't know if this approach for confronting people properly should be used in a violent and abusive relationship. I'm not trained or experienced with that, but I know there are different ways and types of support you should seek to leave that situation safely. Seek help if you are in an abusive relationship.

Everyone should immediately close their mouth and leave any situation changing from confrontation to conflict, especially if there are indications of danger. But in non-abusive relationships, don't be afraid to have a confrontation. You cannot be unwilling to confront someone and be in a relationship with them. Period. Confrontation is best fed sober, calm, and assertive with the best intentions in mind for both of you. It is honest, direct, concise, and straightforward. Don't dilute it with details; that is a conversation. You can discuss the confrontation if the person is receptive and wants to listen. If not, don't engage in conversation; commit to it later. It's usually best to let them process the confrontation for a little while. People often first react defensively but will drop it, given a little time. Don't let yourself counter-react emotionally if you can help it; again, that is a fight. Engaging in a fight will undermine your positive influence. This isn't a person you want to defeat; this is a person you are trying to align with and unite.

When you are showing someone you care about them in this way and are interested in them, but also that you have rules of what you will accept from them, you are successfully influencing them in a positive way. They are responsible for themselves and accepting your boundaries to be accepted by you. You do the same for them, and you both have reciprocity. You then have a solid foundation for a relationship. And it feels good for everyone.

Ways to positively influence the person I'm letting loose from my control:

____

____

____

You may not be good at this exercise at first. That's a great indicator that you must practice it until you are incredible at it. Do it every day if you can, and in a short time, it will only take a minute or two. Every day, transfer your monthly answers and create a new daily objective. You do it and keep your commitment. At the end of the month, take a minute to question the results. Then, make a new list if you need to.

I have refined this exercise to be optimally effective and efficient. It will guide you to discover change in many of the most critical ways. You will rapidly notice your environment becoming friendly; things start going in your favor; your reactions and emotional responses will become steady; you will become more focused and intentional. You will be at the helm of your life with a clearer view ahead.

A person isn't ready to hear about finding out what they truly want until they are in this state. But, since I can't follow up with you at the right time, I'm going to tell it here. Remember this, or make a note to re-read this part after you have a clear view if needed.

The main reason it's difficult to understand **why** you may not know what you really want is because you identify with the things you THINK you want. We build identities around desires and create desires around identities. Much of which was advertised to us somehow to be accepted by our peers. It's scary and painful to threaten to kill a part of yourself or let go of who you think you are. It's primitively and biologically frightening and painful for a social creature to risk being an outcast. But it shouldn't be so scary, especially in our incredibly evolved society of creative sophistication.

Logically speaking on this idea, Alan Watts said that there can only be two reasons why someone doesn't know what they really want.

1. They already have it.

2. They don't know who they really are.

Man! If you hear that at the right time in your life, you will never be the same!

Those words have been ringing in my ears for over twenty years. This is an enormously complicated and interrelated set of human problems reductively explained in a handful of words we can understand at many levels. It is a philosophical equation of great substance. So, what do we do with it?

Ask yourself, "Who am I?". Don't try to answer with your mind, or you'll activate your ego. Just let that question ring out within you and observe the truth as it arises, however it arises. Do not fear the truth; it is where all your power resides. Go deeply into the truth.

Recall that I discussed spending time with yourself and

meditating or being present without thought and distraction. I had you create space to experience yourself and practice being aware of your body. I had you look into your eyes in the mirror and be honest with yourself. I asked you to care for yourself. These are all general practices to start opening doors to knowing who you are. There are many more, and you will create your own. As you start doing more of this regularly and consistently, it will become how you are and how you think. You will notice a growing affection for yourself and for people and things you already have in your life. Speed this up by practicing expressing your genuine gratitude regularly when you feel it.

You will also notice the growing burden and distaste for things you have in your life that you do not want as much as you previously thought. The farther you go down this road, the more you will accelerate, and soon you will be flying effortlessly. You will know you are at the point of lift-off when letting go of things feels good, and knowing what adventure you want next is exhilarating. One way to measure your progress is to compare it to your genuine, selfless desire to lift others without validation. I'm not going to explain that; you will have to experience it for yourself.

Now that you know about changing your mind and how to figure out what you want to change it to, let's get to work on some tangible things.

YOUR VISION

You now know what it means to change your mind and how to discover what you really want. Now, it's time to create a vision for yourself. This vision is the person you will become in the near future. This person will be a more accurate representation of your true nature. This step forward is most often neglected. This is actually the only step you can qualify as forward in time. It is crucial that you give your vision all the effort you have. And why not? It's a truly rewarding and fun exercise. It is also the activity that will yield more inspiration for you.

I promised in the introduction that you could have that youthful sense of possibility and inspiration. Your vision creation is the process of awakening that sleeping flame within. Most importantly, regularly reimagining your vision is the way you will notify and direct your powerful unconscious to select and solve the variables that you don't have the conscious cognitive ability for.

At any given moment, there are thousands, if not millions, of variables and possibilities right in front of you. Almost anything is possible at any moment. It's easy to forget that fact because our conscious minds conveniently reduce the possibilities around us to just a few we can think about. It reduces things to the variables we are focusing on or notice as significant in some way. Much of this book is about taking control of the few variables we have in our view. However, creating and experiencing our visions is the way we put the correct variables in our view to make possible what we want most.

A vision is a straightforward, powerful, and functional tool that is complicated in its mechanics. But just like any other magnificent machine, you don't have to fully understand the mechanics of how it works, just that it does. As I explained at the beginning of this book, you don't have to fully understand how a car works mechanically to use it practically. So, let me give you some evidence that a vision does work. Also, as I said before, if we can't easily and quickly experience something, like a future vision influencing our relationship with reality, then we need to understand how it works to believe that it does.

We know that our perception is limited, and our sight is our most capable and preferred sense. As philosopher Alan Watts believed, our perception is like a flashlight in the darkness of tremendous goings on around us. We can't pay attention to everything around us, only to what we aim our flashlight at. We only knowingly interact with what we see. What we see is entirely dependent upon what we are looking at. What we are looking at is influenced by what we notice that is significant to us and thus has meaning. Holding a vision is the action of intentionally aiming your flashlight in search of the things that will make what you want possible. It illuminates what you need and reveals what you are looking for.

Have you ever bought a vehicle that seemed unique, only to then notice many vehicles similar to it all around you? My first new vehicle was a blue Jeep, and I swore I couldn't remember anyone owning one like it near me. For some reason, that uniqueness was important to me. Over the next week of driving it, I was surrounded by pretty much the same blue on every kind of SUV imaginable. And I saw Jeeps the same as I was driving a dozen times, at least. It was even more noticeable because of something called a Jeep wave. People who buy this brand of vehicle all wave to each other. I was forced to wave at some jerk every few minutes while driving my "unique" vehicle. Even worse, I discovered that someone in my apartment building owned a Jeep of the same exact model and color and had been keeping it in the small parking lot.

I asked her about her blue Jeep, and she confirmed that she had been parking it there for about a year. How was this possible? By most standards, I am an astute observer with a good memory, but I had never noticed this Jeep before. Or, more specifically, I had never noticed this vehicle's particulars. It wasn't previously significant to me that it was a Jeep or that it was blue.

Or you may have had this experience with a shirt, outfit, or something else. Of course, all those people didn't go out and buy the thing because you did, although it can seem strangely like that. Your vision has changed. You are pointing your flashlight of perception at the presence of things with the same qualities as something that has become significant to you. This effect isn't just because there are a few obvious things around you that you don't notice. It is because there is such a tremendous and unfathomable number of ever-changing things moving around you that any of them can be evident if you notice them. You can only aim at a few things at a time. You are selecting what to aim at in every moment.

You have probably noticed that after getting a new job, you start seeing more evidence of that industry. You go to a new gym, church, or club and find out that you already know people who go there. The point is that our perception is our access to reality. But it is so far from complete and limited that it's difficult to comprehend. It's better to think of your perception as a primarily unconscious focus. This exercise seeks to make the perceptive action more voluntary. Much the same way as breathing is unconscious, but we can voluntarily take control.

Holding a vision is how you direct that mostly unconscious focus and bring what you need to see into the light.

If you want to be an influential leader of other people, you must have a vision and impart it to others. If you have employees, children, or anyone else who just doesn't seem able to see what you think is important, they simply don't share your vision. If you want to sell someone something, but the buyer doesn't see its value, they simply don't share your vision. You are responsible for that. But before we get ahead of ourselves, we are focused on creating a vision for our lives. You can use this skill later to create visions to impact others. But, for now, let's keep the flashlight focused on you.

Let's get started while I'm explaining things. You'll need an old-fashioned pencil and paper for the first part. Get yourself alone and quiet your mind of chatter. Practice your meditation for a bit.

Once you are steady, think of what you really want most. It may not yet be clear. That's okay; this practice will help clear it up for you. What you want most could just be a feeling so far, and that's great. Search for that feeling of meaningful inspiration that I mentioned before. What would you want when no one can see or hear you? Ask yourself, "Would I still want it if no one ever found out and there was no external reward to be had?" Use the presently aware self who isn't making judgments. Hold it for a while, and when it is strong, open your eyes and write the rest of these sentences.

I want to be . . . I want to feel . . . I want to have . . . This is the brainstorming part, so don't try to write good sentences; slop the words or phrases down like a list that comes to you from your place of greatest, most honest personal desire. If you start thinking weird thoughts or feeling other emotions, pause and meditate to a steady place again. When you are back firmly in your feeling of what you want most, continue writing. Don't erase anything unless you know it came from the wrong place, or in other words, you know you don't really want it. Maybe you wrote down something someone else expects or wants from you, like your parents, spouse, or boss. Maybe you wrote down something your ego thinks you should be but is afraid you aren't. Be honest with yourself about what you really want, and trust in yourself more than anyone you have ever known. Don't stress; you can't get this wrong. You will find out shortly in interacting with your vision the accuracy of the personal value of your choices. And they aren't permanent; you can and will change them. You will have to test them.

If you have written several things for any of the three lists, prioritize them by importance. This is a hierarchy of actionable personal values. Now, write a rough draft paragraph in the <u>present tense</u> that includes all these things that flow more like a statement. Use the items from your list in priority order. For example, "I <u>want to be</u> an excellent father" changes to "<u>I am</u> an excellent father." At the end of this, you will live out this short story you are writing, first in your imagination and then in life. So, in your vision, you presently are the things on your list, even if you aren't yet to some degree in life.

You are imagining the future as if it were now. This is creation. It is different from lying to yourself. You aren't pretending to be these things from your list and attempting to convince yourself they are true if they aren't. Instead, you are planning to be them while aware that you are not yet and practicing being them with a forward intention. For example, you don't tell yourself you are a great public speaker because you pretend to be in your vision. Instead, you tell yourself I have an opportunity to become a great public speaker, and I am practicing doing that and having that experience in my vision. This distinction illuminates what you need to improve to get there. If you speak loudly and articulately from your diaphragm in your vision but don't do that outside of your vision, you now know what you need to practice with your body. Furthermore, it won't be as unfamiliar to you as it would have been because the experience of speaking that way in your vision is very real, even though it isn't tangible. You can now more easily bring that vision to life and make it tangible.

Most items from your brainstorming list can be true to any degree at any time you choose. But those changes don't always stick so easily and require repetition and practice to become part of your personality. This exercise is the change, repetition, and practice for your alterations. Obviously, any material things you have in your vision that are absent from your current life aren't going to appear in your ownership just because you imagine them instantly. However, they will come into your view soon enough, along with the conditions to obtain them if you really want them.

Back to your vision. Finish your short rough draft of present tense statements of who you are, how you feel, and what you have in your ideal vision of what you truly want. Don't try to force it into an eloquent story. If you aren't a skilled writer, that's okay. Just make your list into basic sentences in order at first. For example, "I am a good father. I feel fulfilled. I have happy children. I am a successful author. I feel inspired and valued by myself and others. I earned a writing award, etc." Easy right? Be even more specific if you can.

Do this in writing for significant reasons. If you are reading this or listening to it with a plan to do this exercise in the future, be wary. You will miss essential elements if you don't write this exercise. Writing your vision is like a scientific spell casting by which you codify your thoughts in relation to your body and reality. You make a thought, place it in the reality of now, and command your hand to move the pencil, like a magic wand, and bring your thought into the tangible world where anyone could see it and understand it. You also then see your own thoughts on the paper with your eyes and decode them back into meaning inside your brain while reading what you have written. This action alone etches your intentions more deeply into your memory and existence than a thought alone. Making thoughts is dropping a leaf in a flowing river; writing is placing a stone.

Now that you have your vision in a paragraph or two have some fun! Read your vision, close your eyes, and start building a narrative. That is forming your vision by bringing together the various conceptual elements. In other words, you are about to build a specific daydream from what you wrote down. This may take some practice and some work. You can test and improve your concentration skills with this exercise. If you find this part difficult, that's a great sign you will make significant progress. Read your draft. Close your eyes and meditate to clear your mind chatter. Don't try to stop thoughts; just let them pass without giving them any attention. When things are quiet, start by envisioning yourself standing naked in an empty white room. Notice in detail how you look. Now, practice changing how you look. Keep to what is within reach. Adjust your muscle tone, shape, skin health, hairstyle, etc. Think of it as your best self. Avoid imagining yourself two feet taller or something absurd. There is absolutely nothing about the basis of your physical body that is very far off from perfection as it is. You are already perfectly designed for the grandest of purposes, no matter your genetics.

Remember, variability is a strength; being different is necessary to make a difference. It is the physical attributes representative of your choices on your body that need attention here. This is a great practice of exercising your power and ability to love yourself as you are, which is a person who can improve and benefit. That will always be true for all of us, and it's something to be grateful for. Notice your opportunities for improvement are not a list of valid reasons to think poorly of yourself or beat yourself up. It's a list of things to be excited about. We have already practiced controlling our thinking and reacting. Now is the time to use those skills to quash thoughts of insecurity and self-doubt. You aren't perfect, and neither am I, but that's the direction in which we are headed. That endeavor is the reason we can genuinely love ourselves.

Now that you have an adjusted view of yourself in your vision, you can get dressed. If you do, pick an outfit that represents what the person in your desired vision would be wearing. Keep practicing envisioning yourself. Try moving around in your vision. Dance if you want to. It's okay to have fun and laugh. I doubt the person in your desired vision is stuffy and boring. What is he or she like? Just make sure you are staying positive. The only way to gain positive results is to envision positive data. Give yourself awesome dance moves, for example. Observe yourself from different angles. Practice until you can hold this simple vision stable. If you are slipping in and out of it or distracting images or thoughts pop in, pause the vision, clear your mind, and restart. Practice a bit longer until you have it.

I'm going to backtrack here a bit. If you find it challenging to do this first part or want it to be easier and faster moving forward, then consider using my entry method. You will revisit this construct and state of mind often, so I have found it best to have a clear and familiar induction. It's a recognizable starting point. I borrowed some parts of this method from self-hypnosis because it works efficiently. I close my eyes, start breathing awareness, and then start counting backward from ten. With every number, I relax more and let go of more. I let any outside sounds push me deeper in. When I get to zero, I am on one knee in my vision construct in front of a chalkboard. The world outside of me is all but gone from my perception. The same chalkboard, in the same room always. I open my eyes in my vision and write my name on the chalkboard. I pay attention to every letter and the minor details as I write. I can see chalk dust floating over my hand, feel the dry chalk in my fingers, and listen to the sound it makes moving across the chalkboard. I then stand up and read my name. Bam, I'm in my vision construct in twenty to thirty seconds.

Before you make this construct difficult, keep it an empty room for now. If you notice that you are looking at yourself and not out from yourself, make that adjustment. In your vision, make sure your visual perspective is first person. In other words, make sure in your vision, you are looking out of yourself through your eyes and not looking at yourself like a camera pointed at you. So, you can look around the room in your vision through your eyes. Hold your hands out in front of you and observe them as you move them around. Look down at your feet and give them a shuffle. Move around or dance as you did before while you are looking out.

All right, that is the basics; from here, you can start designing your room. While you are in your vision, ensure you hold the concepts from your vision draft. The *I have* things are pretty simple, but the *I am* and *I feel* may need close attention. Your attention is isolated in your vision. There is nothing to distract you other than yourself. You may be surprised to find yourself being distracted or criticized still. Fight to win that battle, and always keep your attention on what you want. In this isolated environment, you unmask the part of you that is working against you. In this room, it's just you and your inner critic. This is your psychomachia, the battle for your soul from the dichotomy of your nature. But here, that weak part of you is exposed and easier to defeat. Take victory and be the authority of your attention, deciding to tend to what you choose for the future. You are now the master of your reality.

When you are in your vision, you must experience being and feeling the desired way to match the vision you wrote. This is a critical designation and practice. You can imagine feeling happy, strong, competent, and confident, even if you didn't feel those things before starting your vision. This may be difficult initially, but you will improve quickly. Take some time in your vision, changing only your basic emotions. Don't change them because of something outside of yourself or some activity. Feel happy, for example, then switch to surprised or aroused, excited, humorous, etc. You can and should be able to feel these things without a reason. You are always the one making these feelings; they don't come from outside you. So, practice even if you are terrible; practice until you aren't terrible at it, and then practice until you are proficient.

This practice will give you the power and skill to adjust and decide your emotions outside of your vision as well. It's like exercising your self-sovereignty core muscles. Feeling specific states and emotions in your vision is real for your body. Your body will experience this vision as if it were happening now. This also will embed in you a sense, or intuition, of familiarity that you can notice outside your vision. So, as you are changing things or going about your life, you will notice when you feel something that reminds you of your vision. Take note of why and do more of that; you'll also do this unconsciously. And that is one quality of the mechanism for how your vision comes to life.

Fantasize about accomplishing being, feeling, and obtaining things the hard way, the right way, or for a righteous purpose. The thing about creating quality feelings is that they are made of quality ingredients. For example, if you steal something instead of earning it, you aren't adding the right ingredients to create feelings of competence or self-worth. So, focus on doing everything honorably to get the best results. The same is true outside your vision as well.

You are the architect from here. You can do anything that relates to your desired vision. I suggest making this first room reliable and familiar. Make a door that leads to more rooms. Make sure to have some windows and a door to the outside. What's outside is entirely up to you. Who is allowed in the vision, and when is at your command? Now go for it. Make that vision you wrote down come to life. Create the narrative stories, simple or complex, of your written vision coming to be. Just be sure to hold to your vision and always be your best self. Don't allow any trash, negativity, or deceit to live there. Have good, clean, and deeply meaningful fun.

Do this daily at first. It's a good practice that starts with meditation and is a meditation anyway. Twenty minutes is plenty, but feel free to go longer. But remember, the real magic happens when you bring it to life. Please don't use your vision as a place of retreat; instead, use it as a place to regroup. You will get good at this quickly. This can be fun and surprisingly powerful.

It's a good idea to go back and edit your written vision if needed after some experience. By imaginatively living out your vision, you may find out that you want it to be different. This is the final step to discovering what you truly want. Great, you just saved yourself loads of time in real life, maybe years. This is another impressively functional element called model-based testing. Our greatest thinkers take advantage of testing models all the time. Maybe you incorrectly thought that all this vision creation stuff was sort of silly and not practical. The opposite is true.

Essentially, in vision creation, we are making a mental model of the concept of ourselves, the framework, and the mechanisms. This is how scientists, researchers, programmers, and artists bring everything to life. You already live with other people's invented mental models, such as supply and demand, the atom, entropy, the law of diminishing returns, democracy, virtually all software, any fictional story, etc. They all exist for real, quantifiably, and practically. You should have one for your life; everyone should. Imaginatively experiencing a model or vision is essential to humans. It's how we turn standing facts into running intentions. It's how we test and understand how something is or will likely be. It is how things come to be for us. So, to be better at anything to do with yourself, you must first be different in your thoughts. If you want that improvement to last longer than those thoughts, you must adopt a model or vision constructed of those thoughts. It then starts to move from subjectively perceived to factually true in reality.

Also, you can make your written vision even more powerful if you take some time to develop it from a rough draft into a good piece of writing. It doesn't need to be overly lengthy or profoundly eloquent. It is advantageous for you to develop it. That means working on putting your thoughts together in a well-organized structure. Be clear, honest, and positive. Think of this as writing additional human computer-like code to change your program. Then, upload this code by visualizing and interacting with it. These changes will come to life right in front of your eyes based on how you write them and experience them.

Now, spend some time experiencing it. Your time in your vision mustn't be just about events and things but also sensory and emotional experiences. For example, if you want to be in or improve any kind of relationship, imagine the two of you doing an activity or having a conversation that goes well. Have it be successful, making both of you feel positive feelings. Pay close attention to those feelings. Relish and bask in the emotions; spend time in the feelings.

Let's say you always wanted to be a captain and own a sailboat. Imagine walking out a door in your construct and looking out at your slip. Take a moment to look at your beautiful sailboat and remember that you earned and deserve it. Step aboard, paying close attention to how the deck gives a little under your weight, the smell in the air, and the warmth of the sun-dried rope as you untie it from the dock. As you push off and start to raise the sail, be sure to feel the way you want and intensely experience it.

Things shouldn't go wrong or feel lousy inside of your vision. If this happens while practicing, keep working on it. Without the skills to consistently create and hold imagined success and good feelings, it is doubtful that you will accomplish those things in life. We are always imagining reality. Period. The quality of reality you can imagine is the quality of reality you experience.

Practice until you can hold it steady. In your vision, you are to become all-powerful, omnipotent, and benevolent. Once you can do that without experiencing intrusive, negative, fearful, or reductive elements, it's time to move on to how to intentionally accelerate your desired changes on the outside for the better.

ALTER YOUR ENVIRONMENT

There is a widely accepted but incorrect notion that we can stay the same but achieve different results in life. However, every single example or shred of evidence supports the opposite notion - that the person changes, and the results follow. That's not even considering the fact that everyone and everything is changing constantly anyway. So, why not make it intentional and directional? New results always follow some change a person makes, such as adopting new ideas, changing perspective or belief, a different routine, additional contacts or friends in one's network, a new skill or tool, a different attitude, a new location, or even something as small as an adjusted focus of attention to find an opportunity. It all starts with a change in the person. So, the inefficient way is to try and change your results without making any changes to yourself first. You can bang your fist on that rock for as long as you want, but it won't break; you will. Then, you will either quit or make a change. It's much more efficient and effective to enact a change in yourself first that you have reason to believe will enable you and move you toward a desired result.

"Yesterday I was clever, so I wanted to change the world. Today I am wise, so I am changing myself" – Rumi.

"First say to yourself what you would be; and then do what you have to do." – Epictetus.

"The universe is change; our life is what our thoughts make it." – Marcus Aurelius.

"Is any man afraid of change? What can take place without change? What then is more pleasing or more suitable to the universal nature? And can you take a hot bath unless the wood for the fire undergoes a change? And can you be nourished unless the food undergoes a change? And can anything else that is useful be accomplished without change? Do you not see then that for yourself also to change is just the same, and equally necessary for the universal nature? – Marcus Aurelius

Now that you can have the desired change from your vision held steady in your mind, you need to create the environmental conditions to complement that change. So, let's identify what environmental conditions are in your control. What's outside of you that you can use? You can use anything in your life that contributes to your identity, thoughts, or actions.

First, you have your regular **Locations of Existence.** These are the epicenters of where you build, interact, and experience most of your life and reality. The most obvious ones are your house, where you work, where you socialize, where you learn, and your mode of transportation. Some of these are now significantly online. Anywhere online that you have a profile and virtually interact is a location of existence as well. It can also be parks, coffee shops, bars, live venues, etc. Any place you visit frequently and interact with people or things. I'm not suggesting you have multiple existences; rather, you exist in different physical locations at different times.

Second, you have all the **Things** within these epicenters of your reality. Your stuff: furniture, decorations, sentimental objects, pets, functional devices, tools, etc.

Third, you have all the **People** moving in and out of these epicenters who are also interacting with their own version of reality.

Fourth and finally, you have your **Routines** that govern a fundamental method for when and how you interact with the locations, things, and people.

The four interrelated elements are your system for manufacturing who you are in the world, and what you can do with it. It is easy to make the mistake of thinking you aren't responsible or in control of your system. That is the same as believing you aren't designing your experience. That false belief leads to feeling like and acting like an apathetic passenger. The results of not knowing that you are responsible and empowered to change your life are dismal. On the other hand, the results of knowing that you are authorized and can change your life are incredible.

It's likely true that you cannot change some things in your life immediately. Don't let that fact foster an excuse not to try and start making some change. Just because you can't completely change it yet does not mean you can't make some change toward a result. You will be surprised by what you can do once you start to take steps and gain momentum. For example, if you want to be a physically fit person but have an injury, disease, or obesity that makes it impossible to run a 5K, that's no reason to give up on exercise. Whatever movement you can do, do it more and get better at it. Get into physical rehabilitation first and gain momentum from there. Maybe you want to be living somewhere else but don't have the resources. Don't give up on that. Start doing something small in the direction of your goal, such as putting 10 percent of your pay toward paying off revolving credit or into savings. Sell anything you wouldn't take with you when you move. Start looking at new places you do want to live and consider trying to increase your income and what that would take to accelerate your goal.

Even if you feel stuck in an undesirable situation, you can change much of it if you try. You can definitely change something, even if it's small. And if you recall, two to four percent is a significant engineering adjustment, so anything is enough. You will find that if you make the changes you can, the ability to make further changes will follow with increased momentum.

If you cannot yet muster the motivation and discipline for more than a small change, that's okay; make that small change. Do that again tomorrow, then do it every day. The smallest amount of motivation can drastically improve your ability to progress in six weeks or fewer. That is the incremental improvement impact. You don't have to have 100 percent motivation and a complete plan. You must point in the right direction and start moving. This is true no matter where you are beginning. No human on Earth has wholly realized their maximum potential. If you are motivated to make a faster change, that's great. I'm certain that you can do this either way. Now, let's do it.

Our first environmental condition is our <u>locations of existence</u>. List yours and look at them. These are the epicenters of where you build, interact, and experience most of your life and reality (Review definition above if needed.) Now, think of yourself as the person you want to be; visualize yourself as the person who would achieve what you want. Meditate on it for a while. Write out additional possible locations of existence you would likely have. Cross off the old ones that are unlikely to fit this new version of you. Try to stay objective while doing this. Don't deal with attachments and emotions just yet. This is just an exercise at this point.

Some choices are obvious, and some are not. For example, if you want to be an artistic painter, then working, studying, or socializing in an art gallery or school of some kind would be an obvious move. But what may not be clear is that other places impact your perspective and inspiration for your art. So, you may decide to get out of a cubicle even if you can't change your career to art. Or possibly choose to ride a bike through new paths and parks to get to work instead of the same bus or car (transport cubicle). Subtle changes are more significant than you think. They are always more significant than what you believe is the most important. Write as many as you can on your list. Lastly, put one prominent ideal place on your list where you would be spending time if you could. Such as on a stage performing for thousands of people. On the top floor corner office of the best firm, or your own company. Living in an immaculate home. Turning wrenches in a Formula One garage. Your online video or podcast studio with millions of subscribers. Any ideal place, even if it seems impossible.

Now, compile your data into a new working list of your current locations that you would keep, new ones you would add, and your dream location at the end. Easy. Now, try it out. Jump right in and start adjusting. Don't worry about the fear of change you may have. That is normal. You can start small if you need to and just make changes that don't require making or breaking long-term commitments. However, you will need to have a way to push yourself to continue to make the transition. Hang your list somewhere you can see it often. If you want something to happen for you quickly, set alarms to check your list hourly as you go through the day. See what happens.

Now that you have your locations of primary existence moving toward alignment with your new vision of yourself, you can look at what's inside them. That is all the things within these epicenters of your reality. Your stuff: furniture, decorations, sentimental objects, pets, functional devices, tools, etc. Change is the key here. You can reset the circuitry of your mind and spark some gene activating complemented with neurogenesis with enough change. It's unlikely that you are able or willing to replace all your stuff. Luckily, that isn't necessary. Usually, people have way more than enough stuff. It's better to reduce your stuff. Your creativity and innovation will be more stimulated with less to work with and be distracted by.

Also, some of who you used to be will need to die off to make room for who you are to become. When you let go of old ideas of who you believe yourself to be, that part of you is dying in a sense. Getting rid of things that represent or support that old identity can be emotionally difficult and possibly painful. Remember that discomfort is an indicator of growth and is what you want. Also, remember that you need to make space inside and outside of you for your new vision. A person without a forward vision can experience loss and emptiness from getting rid of identities and things. A person with a worthwhile vision will experience the same event as growing space and opportunity. Keep your vision firmly placed in your mind.

Likely dealing with your things will be the most significant task in your living area. It is best to change everything around with a complete reorganization. Use the garage cleaning technique. Take one room at a time per day. Clear the room as best you can. Then, as you start putting stuff back in, focus on making it different and aligned with your new vision. Don't forget to consider your wall hangings and decorations seriously. If you find out that you can't handle this yet, that's okay. Keep up the other practices and just change anything you can toward your vision. Don't let any amount of failure become a defeat by quitting. Remember, failure is the only way to success. It offers a challenge to struggle through and overcome. This is what you want. You can do this no matter how many small victories it takes.

If you live with other people, obviously, you should only overhaul space designated as completely within your right to do so. For shared space, you are going to have to negotiate with the people you live with. That is a great opportunity to practice articulating your vision, being forthcoming and honest, and possibly dealing with uncomfortable conversations. If you do this well, you will pique their interest, inspire them, and even discover some desired changes they may like to include. Now, you have a reciprocal relationship moving forward together. That is unity, and there isn't anything better to have in a relationship than that.

The more change you desire in yourself, the more change you need to make in your environment. Hold your new vision in your mind. Prioritize the things that you believe fit that vision somehow, and only reintroduce those things. Don't allow yourself to think of other things. Use your new strengthened skill of sustained intentional thinking. Meditate to become presently aware and focus your mind on this singular enterprise, just like we previously did with the color blue. Stop and reset your attention and intention if you get distracted while interacting with your things.

As you reassemble your space, be cautious not to reintroduce your favorite tools of distraction. For example, consider whether you want a TV or gaming system in this space. If your vision of who you want to be doesn't happen by passively watching hours of television, you should be terrified to have one in there. Try to focus on productive functionality. Don't make conditions that require you first to apply effort to use something important to you. If you have a writing area, a meditation space, a music or painting area, etc., make it accessible and ready to use. Trust in yourself to embrace and adapt to these changes. That is what you are looking forward to, after all.

Don't try to make a place for all your stuff. Make a space with only the right stuff. The things that don't make the cut and are left over need to be split into two categories. If something doesn't serve your new vision, and you haven't used it for months anyway, don't put it back. Box it up to be recycled, sold, or disposed of. Second, there may be things that don't fit, but you can't get rid of them for sentimental reasons, or you believe you may need them in the future for a good reason. Box those up, label them well, and store them safely out of sight.

Cluttering your existence with things that are not regularly of service to you is no use. Besides, you want to have open space in your new arrangement. Open space in your living area is available space in your existence. Space holds the dominant energy in the universe. Think of it as blank pages for character innovation and emotional creativity. New and great things require space for them to be created. Now that you have your new, clean, orderly, functional, and exciting location, take a long, hard look at it. Ask yourself, "Is there anything essential to my new vision of me that is missing?"

If you need a functional tool to accomplish your change, that is the priority. For example, you'll need a guitar at some point to become a guitarist. The second priority for adding stuff is the look and feel. Does the space look and feel like you do in your vision of yourself? You can change that up with little or no money, especially if you have sold any unneeded stuff. Get creative and thrifty. Search "thrifty decor ideas" on any browser, hashtag, or social media search bar for endless ideas. Or, if you have money to invest in your new vision, use it wisely. More isn't better.

We must give a special mention to your closet and any self-preparatory areas. These unique epicenters have a huge impact and reach far into your existence. The way you choose to present yourself to you and others is highly impactful. You must be intentional and skilled at this with as little effort as possible. Even better, you should enjoy and look forward to dressing up your body with creative enthusiasm. This is a great place to make a significant change in who you are. Your wardrobe is an armory of your visible identity. Your presentation to yourself helps change how you perceive yourself and shows that to other people. Have a high-quality large mirror. Please place it in good light that's bright enough to be honest but soft enough to be favorable. Try different bulbs or a lamp; get it just right. Give considerable effort to setting up these areas and what is in them.

Do something as close to this method as possible with all your locations of existence as you are able. Clearly, you won't be redecorating your favorite coffee shop, but now you can see some of the criteria for choosing one as your favorite. You can reorganize small places such as work drawers, cars, and digital devices. Change as much as you can.

Next, you need to observe and take inventory of who is moving through your locations of existence. Everyone is essential, and you will benefit from being kind to everyone. That doesn't mean you should engage with everyone. You only have a finite amount of time and energy to interact with others. So, you should make these choices intentionally. There is nothing unkind about politely saying "no" in some way. It is kinder to be polite and honest than to play games. Be the one who decides to approach people.

You are looking to intentionally alter your social structure to fit your new vision of you more closely. Look for people who may fit with that vision or who would have something in common with you relevant to your new focus. Approach new people of your choosing. This puts you in the driver's seat of socialization and makes you unavailable to passengers you would otherwise have to say no to in some way. Before you start approaching people as an intentional practice, be prepared.

Be cautious of physical attraction. Much of it is unconscious and can subversively influence your direction and efforts. There is nothing intrinsically wrong with being attracted to someone, but it does seem to have a way of increasing our perceived value of them and their ideas. That is less objective and will have less utility. The attraction also dips into our unconscious motivations that can influence us to change our behavior unintentionally. That sure doesn't help with holding an intention. Suppose you meant to be meeting a bunch of competent people at an event but catch yourself standing near one person for a long time, laughing loudly at their mediocre jokes. In that case, you may be under the influence of your unconscious attraction to them. Be aware if someone fits into your vision or if you are just attracted to them. Break the seduction and stick to your intention as often as you can; this is correcting course and governing yourself. I am not speaking in the realm of getting into a romantic interaction here, although if that is something you aim to do, you will probably find some of these skills useful.

Be prepared by possessing an excellent working knowledge of interpersonal communication concepts. Interpersonal skills are relational channels of sending and receiving communication. These pathways are the conduit of all reality, especially that which originates outside of your head, otherwise known as new information. How well you can use this conduit will directly correlate to your impact on other people and the world; it also determines how much impact they can have on you. You may not be as good as you believe at communicating with others. Or, if you feel insecure about your skills, learning how these skills work and practicing them will give you confidence and competence. You should have an understanding of encoding and decoding communication. You should also be aware of how you balance discovery and self-disclosure. Just a few hours of learning the fundamentals of interpersonal communication can change your life, but more is better.

It is endlessly beneficial to invest effort into interpersonal communication competence. Read a couple of books on it and practice. Or even taking a class is worth the time and money. You cannot expect a quality exchange or output without a quality conduit. If you don't have a suitable conduit to affect or be affected by external reality (that which is happening outside of your mind), then you will be the only one who understands your vision or even knows how brilliant you are. You are also not properly receiving the remarkable intelligence coming at you.

What is happening inside your head is subjective reality: your interpretation, perception, and experience of what is objectively real. You don't have direct access to much or any objective reality, even though it may feel as if you do. We must go through pain-staking processes as humans to get a glimpse of objective reality that is free from our biases, expectations, egos, etc. These processes include the scientific method, mathematics, meditation, philosophy, logic, etc. Then, to exchange these observations or ideas about them, we must effectively communicate and understand other people. The better you get at communication coming in and going out, the more empowered you are to align your subjective experience with the truth. Be sure to have the basics covered, at least.

Be honest and forthright with people and look them in the eyes. We all have a degree of biological desire for social acceptance. If you combine that desire with our requirement to display a persona of ourselves and throw in a bit of self-consciousness or insecurity into the mix, we can easily feel compelled to make a disingenuous presentation of ourselves. In other words, you probably want people to like you, but you are somewhat afraid they won't, and you are the author of your presentation to them (persona). It's tempting to present yourself differently than you really are in an attempt to convince them to like you. But that false persona isn't an accurate representation of you, so resist that. You know when you aren't being honest. You may not always know what the truth is, but you always know when you are lying.

Remember, you aren't looking to be accepted by everyone. You are trying to align with the right people to carry your vision forward. Finding out who you don't mesh with is just as important as finding who you do align with. That means you will have poor interactions. You shouldn't get all in your feelings about that. You should only feel pleased that your genuine presentation efficiently identified someone who will not fit into your vision of you. Kindly and quickly let them go from your experience. Don't waste one second trying to change their mind about anything.

Know how to listen first and foremost. It is a skill almost no one is nearly as proficient as they believe. Listening is also the most powerful tool you have for positively influencing others. Being heard may be the thing that people desire the most in this world. If you can show someone you understand them deeply, you become important to them. You'll get a higher priority from them for reciprocity in various ways. This is how you encourage others to contribute to you and what you care about, especially those positioned above you.

Test your listening comprehension and decoding/encoding skills by repeating a summary of what someone just said to you and noticing how they respond. This helps you find out from them how well you listen. Learn the skill of listening and practice it often. Read up on it in your interpersonal communication studies. This is a specific skill that can change your life.

Another amazingly effective practice to develop your listening skills is note-taking. Most of us abandon this practice after school. However, the practice of taking notes works very well at learning content and developing and profoundly honing your listening skills. Listen to a video or recording of someone talking and take notes. Stop after five to ten minutes and replay the recording again while reviewing the quality of your notes. Notice what you missed, what you got right, and what you misunderstood. Try listening to something easy at first. It will be interesting and familiar to you. Then, challenge yourself by listening to something more difficult that you know little about. Challenge yourself further by taking quality notes on someone or something you disagree with. Try to hear them accurately; it is more difficult than it may seem. This practice will make you an expert listener and a highly desirable person for others to want to talk with.

When someone likes speaking with you, offer an opportunity to start a relationship of some kind. Never leave a quality interaction without suggesting you stay in touch. Many people are afraid of doing this as something like the fear of closing the sale.

Well, there is the possibility of rejection. It is improbable you will be overtly rejected. The person on the other side of a good interaction desires your acceptance and fears rejection as you do. It is in that way we are built to be social. Most people are polite and fear confrontation, so they probably would take your proposition and reject you privately by simply not reaching out anyhow. Have a physical or digital card to give someone. Have a standard statement to offer, so you don't need to create one on the spot. For example, "It was nice talking with you. We should do it again; here's my card." Apply eye contact and a smile. Leave the interaction decisively and confidently when it's closed. Don't linger; move forward.

One thing you will notice about your interactions with people is that your life has different types of people and relationships. I recommend adopting general modes of communication types to fit each situation best. With strangers or acquaintances, it's best to quickly decide what culture they are most influenced by. Don't be afraid to ask good discovery questions to find out. Don't assume they understand things the same way you do. Let them know you are making sure that you are genuinely trying to understand them. Don't forget that people value a deeply interested, genuine person very much. Stay aware of where they are coming from. That is to say, what things will mean to them from their cultural perspective. If someone identifies most with a culture you know least, listen and ask questions more than talk.

Your interactions with people closest to you will be different as you change. They will observe you behaving differently and doing things toward your vision. Also, your new sustained thinking will affect the topics of your conversation with them. Your friends and family have a historical account of who you were and what you were about. So, they have expectations and assumptions that are ever-present during communication, which you also do for them. These are the people who you need to handle the most delicately as you change. They will likely resist your change and may try to disrupt it to different degrees and for various reasons. They probably won't do it on purpose. In any case, you need to have an expectation and plan. The result you want is to keep these people close to you and improve your relationship with them to support your changes.

So, they will need to accept your changes. That is up to you at first, not them. Being upfront with them is best. Let them know that you want to make some changes for the better and you want them to support you. That may be a weird conversation for you to have with someone you share history with, but it will help. Later, when they see you doing things outside their expectation, they will know why and better understand what is happening. If you can get them looking for ways to understand and assist, you will be even more empowered. Work toward that. You may be surprised by your positive influence on them and their positive impact on you. Or it's possible that you may be surprised to learn how terrible their intentions toward you are. If a person close to you actively seeks to diminish you for any reason, it will be obvious as you try to improve in front of them. You will discover the quality of a relationship when you properly try to improve it. In any case, improving it will be worthwhile.

The people closest to you are the most important other than yourself. They are the most solid elements of your reality and existence. They are the witnesses and quantifiers of your life. Don't let anything less valuable than your survival get in the way of these important relationships. Your survival depends on the ability to engage in meaningful growth. Nearly anything is forgivable except when someone hinders or prevents you from improving. They are killing you, in a sense. So, if someone will not let you change and rise, you will have to sacrifice that relationship, at least temporarily. That sacrifice will be like cutting off an infected finger to save your life. It is at a great cost and causes much pain, but it's necessary. I wish I could make it sound easier, but that wouldn't be the truth.

As much as we may not realize to what degree other people are hindering us, we often don't realize how much we mimic people. We are well adapted to mimicking others and will do it whether we intend to or not, especially with prolonged exposure. The more you engage with someone, the more you imitate things about them. It is one of the primary ways we learn complex cultural skills and create identities.

So, people around you can hinder your growth explicitly by trying to stop you or implicitly because you pick up their bad habits accidentally. You are still in control and responsible for other people's effects on you because you are the one who decides who is in your social circle and who receives your time and attention. You are deciding who gets to be close to you, which has real consequences. It's up to you to make that work for you instead of against you by intentionally matching the company you keep to the vision you hold. What to do about it, then?

Let's hone these ideas with some simplistic precision and make them practical for use. Notice specifically that people either hurt you or help you change. And people have either positive or negative qualities for you to mimic in so much as they complement your desired vision of yourself. So, in both ways, you have the most power of positive self-influence in who you choose to be around and how long you choose to be around them. That is a generally accurate assessment. Be intentional with this. If you are among shit, you will smell like shit. If you are among flowers, you will smell like flowers. However, you can grow flowers in manure better than anywhere. You can inspire positive change in other people, especially in how they behave toward you. But it is difficult, limited, and requires costly work and a strong foundation, especially if they have no desire to change. So, reserve that effort for the people who you most need to keep in your life, such as your family or the people you live with. You must let the other bad influences go for now.

For now, immerse yourself in only the right locations, the right things, and the right people. Doing this will positively accelerate your evolution far more than what you can do alone in the same old external reality fighting against you. This intelligent and intentional alteration of your outside reality super-stimulates your ability to adapt and change. Trust in yourself to adapt. You will adapt, and you'll do it very well. And you will get better at it every time you make a move.

Let's make some moves.

SEW THE ALTERATION

Altering our environment has altered our locations of existence, the things within them, and how we interact with the people moving through them. We are almost done, but there is one last thing that will facilitate the ability to sustain change toward your new vision. Finally, you have your routines that govern a fundamental method for when and how you interact with locations, things, and people. Your routines govern how you regularly interact with reality. They are the most crucial element to accomplishing incremental or lasting improvement. Routines and habits are also purported to be the most challenging thing for a person to change. Unfortunately, so far, I have found that to be true.

However, trying to deploy sustained awareness of your bad habits and undesirable routines that need to be changed means that you are also stimulating your chances to engage in them by increasing the frequency with which you are thinking of them. That is a problem. Unfortunately, that paradox is present. Usually, we can use awareness to disempower subversive forces of our psyche. For example, when we meditate to observe our thoughts, the emotion tied to them dissipates. Or, when we face fear, it diminishes. Fortunately, we have incredible human discoveries and subsequent proven technology that can reliably replace many of our routines and assist in our unconscious retraining.

Humans have discovered how to measure the future with time, communicate to our future selves, and plan to engage in a future existence. We can decide, in advance, exactly when and how we will experience reality and engage in life with stunning accuracy. And now, most of us carry a highly developed technology that does nearly all the work for us. I'm talking about having a schedule on a digital calendar. That set of discoveries is not something to take for granted. I know that seems obvious, and people generally think they do this well. But we don't. I thought I did too, but I didn't do it well until I learned it from someone else. I have since made improvements.

A good personal calendar will have places to be, activities to do, and cues for thoughts and feelings you want to have. This kind of future map will help you hold your intentions and move you toward your vision hour by hour or even minute by minute at times. Creating a scheduled calendar is like mapping unknown territory based on what you can predict from what you have experienced so far. The more detailed and specific that map is, the better it will work. Clearly, you can only be specific and detailed about what you know for sure. And you also know for sure that you will need the flexibility to deal with what you don't know.

Here is how mine started for today- if you like examples:

5:45-6:00 am - Wake up, move around, breathe deep, don't touch the phone, look into the dim light on the horizon while coffee is brewing, and feel the peaceful anticipation of the possibilities of the coming day.

6:00-6:20 am - Read over the latest vision while sipping coffee, then meditate. Clear mind first, then enter vision.

6:20-7:20 am Edit a chapter of *We Aren't Who We Are* - Stay self-aware and hold your intention to speak the truth as clearly as possible that may be useful for people - sit up straight and breathe deeply.

7:20-7:30 am Wake up Luna (my seven-year-old daughter) for summer camp. Be enthusiastic, show love, and make eye contact with her. Encourage her to get herself ready as much as she can and report back when she is done.

Feed the dogs.

7:30-8:00 am Do "Morning Routine" (currently, it's a mix of

yoga, calisthenics, and some resistance training for muscle activation while staying present and aware.) Begin with five minutes submerged in a cold-water bath (currently 43 degrees F.). Focus on letting the intense sensation just be that, and don't let it turn to suffering. Control reactivity. Let it flow through you and cleanse out any weakness of character.

8-8:30 am Shower and warm up while thanking yourself for showing up for yourself today by choosing a challenge and struggling through it honorably. Congratulate yourself for that victory. Get dressed and packed for the day.

8:30-9:00 am Give my wife and oldest daughter my full attention, affection, and positivity – Take Luna to Camp and make the ride fun and engaging, helping her orient herself toward looking forward to any challenges to overcome.

9:00 am Set your intention in line with your vision and enter your workday self-aware and optimistic.

...continues on until sleep.

There is some fashionable idea of not living as a slave to a schedule. But if you are the one creating your schedule that guides you to what you want, you are not a slave. As soon as you realize that you have planned for everything essential in the future, life is much less stressful. You will be much more able and likely to be spontaneous. You will know precisely what will be affected by spontaneous activity, so the anxiety of the unknown won't haunt you. If you aren't trying to remember all the things, big and small, that need to be done, you free up a ton of mental energy. In fact, if you have a good plan, you won't have to worry about remembering a single thing that needs to be done. What would you do with that freedom?

A scheduled plan also prevents you from attempting multi-tasking, which isn't a productive strategy. You have a finite amount of attention you can give at any moment. If you concentrate on only one thing, it receives 100 percent of your attention. Giving 100 percent attention to things is what you want to practice. Multitasking is diluting your available attention by dividing it among multiple things. That is inefficient and produces a lower-quality interaction. Give each task on your schedule as much attention as possible as if it is the only consideration in the world at that moment. This may be obvious with initiatives on your calendar, such as finding a way to reach new clients, completing a research project, or finishing a complicated task at work. But it's also true for seemingly mundane things such as getting a haircut.

A haircut or something else seemingly insignificant can be perceived as something you must do or get through to get back to important things. Or it can be viewed as an opportunity. With a good, complete schedule, you don't have to think or worry about anything else in the future or the past during a haircut. You can be presently aware and deeply connected to yourself, other people, and your environment. Often, the most significant learning or connections are made in the places we wouldn't expect. But they can only be discovered if your attention is available. If nothing pops up relevant to your vision, you will still have a meaningful experience free of anxiety. You'll never feel like you are waiting in the sense of wasting time. Even if you end up in a situation where all you can do is wait silently, you will appreciate the reprieve and enjoy spending time with yourself.

Whenever you are asked to wait longer than your available time, you can simply look at your calendar and make an emotionless decision to make more time or not. Go back to your priority list from the chapter *What You Really Want* if you need to. You will know exactly what you are giving up. If you are forced to wait longer than your available time, like in a traffic jam, it won't be a catastrophe. A glance at your calendar will show you precisely what is going to happen in the future as a result, and you can calmly take appropriate action if needed.

Give the present moment all your attention. You can accomplish things more efficiently by putting them in a line instead of attempting multi-tasking because you can do them with remarkable speed and proficiency. A calendar is linear through time. It is putting everything in a line to do them one at a time. I also use task lists inside of the calendar for activities requiring small tasks to be completed efficiently. This is different from a "to-do list" for the day. Instead, it looks more like:

-From 12:30 - 1 p.m., create a full sequential task list needed to complete the project from 1 p.m. to 4 p.m. -This is a method to make the complicated project more efficient by making an instruction manual first.

The only time I use a "to-do list" otherwise is to remember things that I may need to put on my calendar. I do think it's a great idea to keep a list of things that pop into my head that I want or need to do. Epiphanies that will help me are valuable. But it's when I go to put them into my calendar that I get to compare their value to my vision in competition with what is already on there. "Do I have time for that?" becomes, "Do I truly want to make time for that?"

When observing my employees, I have seen an unbelievable amount of wheel spinning, as I call it. That is running around partially doing things without much focus or quality, switching to other things they forgot were the priority, and then trying to switch back or sideways, etc. That sort of method can make two hours of work last ten hours with less quality and significantly more stress. Even worse, we don't usually notice that we are doing it or just how inefficient we are. If you have employees with tasks, give them this gift of proper planning and execution to apply additional benefits to your bottom line.

What goes on a scheduled calendar? Most people will say to include places you must be at a particular time. True, but that is about 5 percent or less of the information of a good plan. The rest is the specifics of what and how you will accomplish that is aligned with your vision and intention. Make your schedule digital and interactive with good tools if you can. Apple or Google Calendars are usually free and allow you to choose what days of the week things repeat. You can put expandable notes in every event to talk to and direct your future self like a guide, leaving clues through the wilderness that has drawn you a map. You can color code things to remind you of their purpose or priority. If you like analog, you can print out your calendar. You can have your phone alert you in different ways, reminding you to stay on the path or correct course.

The only notifications I get on my phone are calls and texts from priority people who depend on me, but every single event on my calendar notifies me. I have space on my calendar to check my phone for other notifications and return other important calls, etc. Minimize vulnerability to distraction from your plan wherever possible. If a stranger needs to get ahold of me, they can wait until I'm available. If it is urgent, it is their emergency, not mine. A life without unnecessary emergencies is called peaceful.

Spend loads of effort designing your plan, and plan to adjust it as you learn from it. Make it incredibly detailed and specific to accomplishing your best future version of yourself. Make your plan something to live up to but not out of reach. On average, I revise mine every six weeks. I update it constantly, but I think about complete fundamental changes every six weeks or so. If you are improving, so should your calendar. If you master your calendar, some of it starts becoming familiar and useless. Push further.

Plan creative time, make-up time, and free time. Those are essential, or your plan will not work. This is one of the two ways you empower yourself to be guiltlessly spontaneous when you get inspired to do something unplanned in the moment; that is a great thing! Simply move what you planned to open space on your calendar for "makeup time." Or eliminate something on your calendar of lower priority for the day to make time to follow your whim. This was one of my favorite advantages of this practice. It's difficult to describe just how much more fun it is to do something off the cuff while knowing you are still on course to your vision. Or even if you give something up, you know exactly what it was and that it was of the least priority.

Advanced tip: Try learning to be more spontaneous by

scheduling time to be spontaneous. I know the concept sounds counterintuitive, but the practice isn't. When the calendar alert goes off, your instructions are to do something out of the ordinary and novel to you. Don't think too much; just do something weird. Such as calling someone you haven't talked to in years, grabbing someone you love by the hand and going for a walk or dance, driving to the nearest nature spot, going skinny dipping, etc. This is a great way to learn to take action to become inspired instead of waiting to be inspired to take action.

When you include make-up time, free time, and creative time in your developed calendar, you will gain critical insight into just how much you can and cannot do within the limits of time. You may have more room than you thought to add some quality endeavors. You may instead discover that you must make sacrifices and stop doing some things. Pay attention to what you learn, and you may solve problems you didn't even know you had. Remember that this is your most important source of power and control. This is the future experience with reality you are writing. You get to choose much of what it is like.

Try to wake up at the same time every day as often as possible. Include what you plan to start that day thinking about. Include how you plan to feel as you described in your vision. Read it when your alarm goes off, and remember why you wrote it. Let yourself feel that way and let go of other feelings. Remember, feelings don't really happen to you; you make them and choose them. You become better at doing this through practice.

As you put together your scheduled calendar, talk to your future self in the notes for events. For example, schedule your eighteen minutes to eat and put something in the notes such as, "Rest your mind, slow your thinking, and focus on . . . " Make important things a priority. That sounds obvious, but it isn't. Most people deprioritize creative endeavors so low they're relegated to doing them only during free time. That thinking is exactly backward for accomplishing progress and innovation of oneself.

I have often mentioned aligning your existence with your new vision. An essential aspect of that is a working knowledge of personal identity. This is the person you imagine yourself to be and all the things that accompany that. We tend to grasp onto, worship, and protect our past identities. We even have developed something to fear, which we call an "identity crisis." But a big part of why we even have an identity in the first place is to have a stable form of ourselves to portray to others for the purpose of socializing. This is our persona or social identity. It is a mistake to cling to your identity for security, especially if you aren't satisfied with it or the results. We know it must change every day because everything it's made of is constantly changing. We also know that without it, you are still you.

If you lost your memory of your identity, you would still exist, but if you lost your life, your identity would not persist. This is the essence of the fear of death. Remember, you are the person that keeps your identity alive. So, we also have the problem of desiring to get great results in life that require a great change but not permitting ourselves to change. By changing our identities, I mean that we allow ourselves to change our minds about who we are and how we are different from others as we gain more information and experiences. Trying to make great positive changes in ourselves while clinging to a past identity are mutually opposed activities. It's like trying to push and pull a door simultaneously. Not only can you never walk through it, but you will also experience frustration. It's also worth pointing out how common it is for us to be displeased with how our life is going or who we are while simultaneously overvaluing our current identity as if it were helping us somehow. That's wearing handcuffs like bracelets.

Instead, consider your identity as a powerful tool you have to help yourself intentionally evolve. Loosen your grasp a bit if needed. Think of your persona as something to create that reflects and expresses the deepest truth you can understand so far. You can make it beautiful. To make more of a difference, you must be different than you are. You must give yourself permission to be different in order to grow, progress, and create different results.

There is good reason to think that your overall identity serves you in some ways. And some parts of it are unchangeable, such as where you are from, your first language, ethnicity, sex, etc. But you are still in control of how you think and feel about these things or if you even do think and feel about these things. I have never seen an example where permanent attributes must be changed to accomplish greatness. However, I have seen countless examples of the way someone views their attributes, which need to be altered to be successful.   There may be a struggle attributed to an unchangeable part of your identity, but now we know that meaningful struggle is precisely what we need anyway. Denying or attempting to change immutable facts in reality or one's biology is unnecessarily dangerous. It is unnecessary because you were born perfectly suited to accomplish your unique contributions to the world through effort.

Much of your identity is already useful and worth keeping for the purpose of moving you toward your vision. You have to decide what to keep and what to allow to change. Base those decisions on what you believe to be true and what has the most utility for accomplishing your vision for yourself. For example, if you wanted to be an exceptional carpenter, you would need to become someone who loves carpentry, interacts with other carpenters, knows the variety of wood, appreciates the tools, wears the leather tool belt, speaks the language, and knows the nomenclature, etc. The moment you think of yourself as a carpenter and you do carpentry, you are a carpenter. Maybe you aren't a good one yet, but you are one in your identity. However, you don't have to become a man if you're not; you don't need a certain skin color, and a full beard might be cool but is not requisite. Think highly of the unchangeable gifts you were given to be unique, but take responsibility for the rest of who you are.

The best rule to evolving your identity is to alter any aspect of your life that gets in the way of you becoming what you truly want and dispense with anything that isn't a good representation of the truth and reality. In the fitness example, it would be anything that gets in your way of being active, an athlete to some degree, or just a physically fit person. Identifying these things will take some emotional honesty and searching. I'm not just talking about obvious practical things. But let's start there.

To be an active, fit person, you will want your life to reflect that. That doesn't necessarily mean going out and buying expensive equipment. It means making your life flow like a functional and efficient athletic body. Trim the fat. Clean out the clutter and disorganized areas of your home, workspace, phone, computer, or wherever you spend time. On a full stomach, organize the hell out of your pantry. Keep healthy and tasty foods. Remove the foods you don't plan to eat. This doesn't mean you can't throw your pants on the floor and eat a cupcake sometimes. Go for it. Just make it the exception, not the rule. Don't give cupcakes and counterproductive behavior much thought one way or the other. Seek to make those thoughts and behaviors obsolete by replacing them with your more worthwhile intentions and initiatives to achieve your vision. Pretty soon, they will disappear from your life on their own if you stay engaged with improvement. This is how altering the environment of your mind is done.

If you are trying not to eat cupcakes, you are thinking about them. I'm guessing by now you are starting to understand why thinking about cupcakes doesn't lead a person away from eating one. That mechanism doesn't work well. We can't do it unless we are strong enough for explicit behavioral sacrifice. That is the goal, but the trick is to sacrifice destructive thoughts for constructive ones so the poor behavior doesn't manifest. We must focus forward instead.

We are always programming our minds with our thoughts. Our mind is constantly influencing changes to our behavior to accommodate the programming. If you get off course to your destination, simply correct course. That means restarting, thinking about and doing the things you want to be doing, and focusing forward. Don't think about the things you are doing wrong. There is no point in feeling guilty about anything for more than a few seconds. Guilt is a dangerous emotion that doesn't serve you. Guilt is a wasp you catch in your hands. Your lesson is learned immediately. Only one result will come from keeping it trapped in your hands. It will sting you endlessly until you let it go or crush it. Letting go is the lowest-risk method. Letting go still requires effort and movement.

A different way of saying this is that a boat captain cannot correct his direction by mainly thinking of where he shouldn't be going. Try looking at a map and finding a destination by thinking and looking only where you don't want to go. You obviously cannot find your destination. The same goes for your life. Give up on that futile method of living and improving. It is that simple, so it is paramount that you are aware and have authority over your mind. An unbridled mind does not stop taking you places; it's more like dropping the reigns of your horse and kicking it in the ribs. It will lead you all over the map, and you will really feel like you are getting somewhere because you are moving and experiencing things. You will never arrive at an intended destination, however.

Don't underestimate the impact of adding a new stimulus to your environment. Join an exercise or activity group to be a fit person. Make new friends and acquaintances who work out or do your favorite activity. This skill is so much easier than it appears. Try just being direct and honest with people about your interest and intention to become their friend. Don't forget they have the same feelings as you, including wanting friends and acceptance. You are doing them a favor when you say, "I think we would make good friends. Here is my contact information." Let them respond. Sure, that may be scary, but say it anyway, and it will get easier. You will see that the right people want to connect with you.

Also, go ahead and change your screen saver or hang a picture of an image that makes you feel active. Wear more athletic clothes. Correct yourself if you start worrying about what other people will think about your changes. You aren't in control of other people's opinions anyway. Don't fret if you feel discomfort about changing. Face these things, and you will adapt. You are the author of your identity in every moment. No one can change it or measure it other than you. Identity creation is your tool, and you are in control of it. It's not the other way around.

I've been using fitness as an example, but you can use these methods with anything.

Speaking of identity and persona, let's address interactions with technology and the social media and social gaming world. This includes VR, AR, AI, and metaverse. Social media is a great reflection of our individual and collective minds. They are instrumental and powerful tools to empower or destroy your life experience. Fortunately, we can turn them off when we want, but that may only be the case for a while. So, it's urgent that we get authority over our engagement now. If you use social media platforms to help you engage in content that positively contributes to the destinations and life results you want, they superpower you. But beware, there are unavoidable and wildly attractive distractions to pull you off course.

I like to think of social media as a huge power tool. You don't want to use a concrete saw to cut your fingernails. For example, if you feel a bit lonely and need support, call a friend or DM one. Maybe it isn't for the best to make a post about it to the public with a depressing image to collect a tremendous amount of sympathy, likes, loves, and emojis, and then check your progress every few minutes.. That's probably too much; it creates an identity that won't serve you well. It creates harmful thought patterns and sends constant instructions to your mind to be as pathetic as possible to deserve this identity. It will likely not make you feel better overall. You are going to risk solidifying your unwanted feelings instead of alleviating them. This is a negative behavior that reduces you.

In this example, flip the script if you want to feel better using social media. Post or engage with positive recognition, gratitude, or simply something you like talking about. Even if you don't feel into it, watch what happens. In a short time, you will feel into it. Then, you will engage and get all the same positive results you would have collected if you started feeling motivated. This way, you get positive results 100 percent of the time and are engaged, motivated, or inspired most of the time. There are those people who must be motivated to act and those who take action to feel motivated. This subtle difference is everything for your net results. This is also the difference between a leader and a follower. You will get to practice this with physical exercise and apply it to many things.

There will be plenty of times you will wake up and feel like shit. It's decision time. You now know what will happen if you spread your shitty feeling, surrender back to your chains, and wait to feel like taking action. Or you will not let your mind craft beautiful complaints and formulate excuses. But instead, you will take action that you know will point you to your destination. It's probably written on your calendar now, and you know you can trust those instructions more than your shitty thoughts. As a result, you will see the motivation and results come to you much more quickly when you create them instead of waiting for them.

After some routine practice, you will understand things this way. You will think things such as, "I need to take a jog or a walk," when you feel lethargic. "I better do something nice for someone else" when you feel hateful or argumentative. You will think, "It's time for me to travel, learn something new, meet some new people," when you start feeling stagnated, reclusive, or uninspired. When you begin to think and act this way, things you once considered a discomfort or something to avoid will now set you aflame. You will have become a captain instead of a castaway. You now have authority. You are now free and able to go anywhere you want in this life at an incredible rate. You will now have less desire to scroll a random social feed; if you do, you will probably be searching for something in particular.

There is much I could say about social media and much we must all learn as we go. Stay aware of what you are doing on social media, and answer, "Why am I doing this?" If you catch yourself getting sucked in, you must break this pattern. Try setting a timer for ten minutes before opening an app. When it goes off, ask yourself, "All right, what am I doing here, and what do I really want to do right now?" You should have some pretty good answers, especially after reading this book. I have found that most of the time, I have no desire to continue using it when my timer goes off. The other times, I am doing something that is taking me toward a destination in some way. Set the timer again and continue. It works because it keeps you aware. If you are aware, then you'll know when you need to correct course. I hope we figure out a quick way to get actionable information about how best to use these things soon. We need it.

DRIVE YOUR DRIVES

What are drives, and why are they important? A drive is what happens before you are motivated to act. At the basic biological level, drives are cravings that motivate us to take action to satisfy a deficiency. This is what keeps us alive and propagating. That is a paraphrased summary of *drive theory of motivation* (Reeve 2018). For example, it is when you feel thirsty, hungry, sleepy, or aroused. This is an observable place to notice our bodies communicating and interacting with our psychologies. Even the most basic things can get complicated when drives move around in human psychology and into our complex personalities. Those are called secondary drives.

My point is that even at the most basic level, we haven't figured out exactly how all this works. And it gets wildly complicated beyond that. So, for now, we need to take what we know as sufficient proof that we have drives, what some of them are, and that they inspire motivation for us. That is enough to know for sure that we need to be aware of our drives and cultivate them to work for us. It's also enough to know that repression of drives will cause us to behave more like wild animals and act unintentionally and potentially destructively.

When a person is unaware of their drives or not in control of them, the drives don't stop motivating the person. Their drives motivate them unbridled and randomly as they respond to stimuli. This is more like how an animal in the wild behaves; however, we aren't wild animals. We are sophisticated in an important way. We can use our intelligence, memory, and understanding of the future to delay gratification in the present to achieve a more meaningful future result. But when we don't use that sophistication, our complex psychology can abstract our motivations in all sorts of weird, inappropriate contexts, some of which are destructive and possibly abhorrent. However, intentionally suppressing drives (trying to stop them from happening) is like stopping steam from escaping with a lid. The steam will always come out somewhere somehow and maybe violently. The difference between delaying gratification and suppressing or repressing drives is found in our judgment and opinion of the drive. If we believe the drive is evil or unacceptable and block it out maybe forever, that is repression. On the other hand, delayed gratification is knowing the drive is natural and acceptable but is less valuable to satisfy than the reward gained for not immediately satisfying it. In delayed gratification, a reward is still on the horizon, and it's better than the one in front of you. It's best if we all try to be aware and accepting of our drives so we can take responsibility and cultivate them.

There is always something we desire, but it will seem to be of lower value as soon as we get it. It is well known in the scientific literature that a measurable drop in dopamine after a reward creates a refractory period that takes time to reset. The anticipation period measures the highest dopamine release. In this way, we can get stuck in a cycle of wanting new consumer products to solve our low feelings caused by the very thing we seek. We want to want and believe we can satisfy that with a reward thing. We satisfy the want and then are dissatisfied without the feeling of wanting. So, we must do it over and over again. The object will never satisfy us; otherwise, we would need only one object for each purpose and simply take good care of it for our whole lives.

Endless satiation cycles can evolve into wasteful consumerism, hoarding, excess hedonism, inappropriate participation in activism, conflict seeking, and worse. It's a repeatedly disappointing and insatiable chase that risks contributing to depression and anxiety in a major way when we don't handle it properly. Picking something of higher value to want and sustaining that anticipation for a longer period of time with a greater challenge to earn it is a much better experience. Like saving for a house instead of buying the shiny, exciting thing that arouses you every couple of days. Or developing a meaningful relationship with someone to share a home with instead of aiming for the quickest bed to share. Developing a skill or education with the time you have instead of the many temptations you could be doing otherwise. A person with a home, a partner, a skill, and education is reaping much greater rewards than the other.

For example, I discovered a mistake I was making when I was young that is shared by many people. I used to want to travel the world like we hear so many people say, but I couldn't afford it and couldn't afford to take off work for a trip. However, on inspection of my monthly checking account statement, I found that I was spending way more money than I expected on things that didn't mean anything to me after I bought them. I remember looking at purchases and being aware of how important and attractive they seemed at the time, but now, less than a month later, many of them meant nothing to me. I wished I could take them back. I wondered if I would trade some restaurant trips, a few brand-name clothes, and a couple of convenience store stops to move me 10 percent closer to a meaningful trip. When I asked that question weeks after getting those things, I answered yes. The trick is remembering that feeling in the moment of attraction and delaying your gratification for something more meaningful.

The thing we usually impulsively desire is to feel good or a good feeling. Getting expedient good feelings isn't the same as feeling good. Getting too many good feelings is often the path to feeling bad overall. Feeling good comes from something more like being honored to be with yourself. That would mean that knowing every thought, word, and action that you have, you still regard yourself with great respect, are pleased to display yourself to the public, and you have kept your agreements with yourself. What we should try to avoid is taking action that feels good only for a moment that doesn't require a challenge to obtain. We most often make this mistake with food, shopping, sex, and entertainment.

Instead of making a purchase with a credit card the reward, make the earning and saving money to buy something in particular the reward. Instead of making easy sex or masturbation the reward, make the chase of seduction and intimacy the reward. Instead of feeling easy entertainment such as TV or social media is the reward, try picking things that require effort for entertainment, such as card games, board games, or a sport. And if you can't do these things for some reason, the best trick is to make yourself do something important to your long-term benefit before you take the easy reward. At least finish the dishes before plopping down in front of the TV. Or read a chapter of this book before you open the next popular social media app.

The important designation here is not to get trapped in a state of wanting that is perceived as a state of lacking or frustration. Instead, learn to perceive the anticipation and challenges themselves as the primary reward. Genuinely being proud of yourself is worth a million pounds of easy pleasure in your psyche. You can do this the whole time you are ascending toward a goal. Honor is sculpted in how you do, not what you do. For example, don't focus on the idea that you can't have restaurant food; if that's your plan, focus on that moment when you move that money to your travel savings account at the end of the week. Congratulate yourself on that difficult victory toward a worthwhile goal, and look forward to doing it again.

The anticipation and challenge are the primary rewards. You have a mission, and it fosters drive. That statement is factually true. You want to foster a strong drive to feel driven. You want to look forward to working toward a thing instead of receiving it. You want to appreciate a feeling of appetite and craving as your catalyst for inspiration, improvement, and growth. Don't kill your desire for anything quickly just because you can satisfy it without much effort. The moment you decide to want things of high value that aren't easy to get, then seek to earn them with effort; you will have everything you need already.

Think highly of your natural drives, enjoy them, and use them as an incentive. Review the section "Love and Struggle" if needed. This is how you flip your state of existence from experiencing lack, tension, and anxiety most of your life to experiencing positive anticipation, ambition, and excitement.

For example, you will feel hungry if you don't eat for a while. Let yourself feel hungry as a positive emotion instead of anxious tension. Know that if you sustain it a little while, food will taste even better. So, the quality and intensity of the reward goes up. Then, take on a challenge of some activity, with the food being the reward at the end. Enjoy the feeling of hunger the whole time and look forward to the reward. Put it in your mind that the better you perform, the more you will reward yourself. Don't let yourself seek to satiate the hunger as a problem that needs solving. It truly isn't an urgent problem unless you haven't eaten for a day or more.

When you make it to the reward, you will enjoy it greatly. You will find that you seek a higher quality of reward. You will desire nourishing foods instead of cookies, for example. That whole experience is so good that you won't want to ruin it by overindulging. Don't eat to the point of feeling stuffed and sick. Leave yourself feeling fueled and look forward to feeling hungry again. As soon as you can make a drive, such as hunger, a positive emotive stimulus, you will want more of it. At this point, you have flipped the script of what the life experience is like between rewards. Then, you can stimulate any drive to have more of it and greater rewards as a result.

Hunger is a very influential drive that you get to experience regularly. So, it is good practice and routine by nature. This is a good place to practice cultivating your drives and having authority over yourself. I became a master of incentivizing myself with hunger in my attempt to manage weight-to-power and stamina ratios in wrestling training. You can develop your skill of self-incentivizing and feeling positive anticipation instead of tension quickly by practicing with your appetite for food. When feeling hungry instead of eating becomes the reward and a positive feeling for you, you may want to increase it in a productive way. You don't want to increase hunger by starving yourself, or you will become weak and unhealthy. After a while, you won't feel more hungry. You will feel weak and less hungry. That is how your body responds and adapts to become more efficient.

To properly increase hunger for nutrition as a physical stimulus more than an emotional one, you need to do strenuous activity with your body. I suggest some kind of muscular resistance. Learn the skill of resistance training. Yes, it's a good practice for anyone and everyone, but you need a routine that fits your abilities and goals. Also, it prepares your body for something even better. Go outside and play, do physical work, or do any productive activity that is physically difficult. It doesn't matter your ability level; do what you can. Go out a little hungry and use your body to move earth, build, cultivate, play, or whatever. Get your heart pumping and your sweat running. Make your muscles burn. We were built for this, and you will feel so incredible that you can't remember why you avoided it. Oh, how that dinner after will taste so good. Show yourself your strength and eat it slowly while you enjoy the sunset. Congratulations, you are alive. Even better, you are incentivized to be alive.

If you keep up this practice and apply it to your other drives, you will start making fundamental shifts in your thought patterns and experience of reality. You already have a powerful incentive to make this shift. You have a choice to feel positive anticipation instead of anxiety, ambition instead of lack, excitement building instead of tension. When this possibility becomes your reality, and you are driving your productivity in this way, success is unavoidable, and inspiration walks with your every step.

Sex drive is similar to hunger in a few ways. It stimulates productivity with some depravity, but it is likely unhealthy and counterproductive to starve for too long. What your timeframes are is for you to figure out. Unlike hunger, the intensity and frequency of sex drive is more varied from person to person and can change throughout the different seasons of our lives. Whatever your timeframe is, use it to your advantage. Sex is one of the strongest motivators and most intense rewards for humans. That is how you should think about it. Avoid feeling like you are entitled to sex or ashamed of it; instead, think about what you can do to earn it and deserve it.

You will find that the things you previously put in your vision and the other exercises in this book are also the best ways to become more desirable, which helps improve your relationship or helps get you in one. As you become healthier and aligned with what you are deeply inspired by, you will become more invigorated, confident, competent, and connected to who you really are. These are the best conditions to genuinely be attractive.

Enjoy your sex drive. It isn't intrinsically bad. Think positively about it. Like all drives, it is dangerous if left uncultivated. You don't want it manifesting at inappropriate times or distracting you from your goals. So, cultivate it and put it to work for you. That means carrying it with positive anticipation instead of tension or anxiousness. Let yourself be excited to reward this desire after an accomplishment toward your vision. Let yourself fully enjoy the reward and receive it guilt-free. Then, seek to increase the drive and keep it stimulated. I'll talk more about this drive in the next chapter.

Be mindful of your drive to be social. Let it motivate you to seek out new groups of people who share a similar vision as you. Join groups about what you are interested in or want to be interested in from your practice of changing your mind. Let your drive to socialize and be accepted give you the courage to speak up and make the right kind of new connections. This method will incentivize your action and stimulate the drive. With every exciting new positive connection, you will gain confidence in seeking out more.

Thirst is a drive that needs to be satiated all the time. Yes, you can survive in today's world without proper hydration, but you cannot thrive to your maximum potential. The risks and costs of dehydration outweigh any possible benefits of using this drive differently. Also, keeping your hydration up consistently lets your body work its incredible magic that solves most of your problems without your conscious intervention. Hydration is a prerequisite to everything for a human. You suck at everything comparatively until you are hydrated. Nine years of cutting water weight for wrestling gave me an experiential insight into the power of hydration versus dehydration. Trust me; you suck; get a glass of water. Seriously though, most people are likely underhydrated.

Also, your drives often get mistranslated from your body to your psychology, so you can feel hungry or sleepy if you are dehydrated. That's a major fail. If you want to test it yourself, try this: start the day with a full glass or two of cool water, no ice. Then, carry a six to nine-ounce cup, fill it with cool water every hour or two of inactivity, and throw it back. Yes, chug it, like medicine. It requires much less focused motivation to quickly drink water one time per hour than remembering to sip it every few minutes. Your stomach is a perfectly designed container for water. Just put it in there and let your body dose it out. During periods of activity, you will want to drink additional water. If you take a stimulant of any kind, such as coffee, you will also need to drink extra water. You also may want to try ditching the stimulant. You might find that you no longer need it. Do this for three days and evaluate your mood, energy, sleep quality, sex drive, hunger frequency, and types of food desired. Try seven days. You may find the results remarkable.

Sleep is another essential drive. Quality sleep is essential. If you have trouble sleeping well, investigate it and seek help. I believe that sleeping fewer hours makes one better at it to a certain degree. You can see from the many sleep studies done on sailors, especially solo sailors, that their bodies adjust to get more quality sleep faster with the constant pressure to do so. However, their performance suffers when sleep times fall below a certain threshold, depending on the conditions. This is true for all of us. Adjust your sleep time to what you think is best; push for quality sleep. Sleep quality is as essential as food, water, and socialization to the quality of your life and results.

Don't assume you are good at sleeping just because you have been doing it your whole life. Make sure you are good at it. FYI, you will be better at sleep if you are physically exhausted by bedtime. That seems obvious, but we all know that feeling when we are tired. We know that our bodies aren't actually exhausted from doing anything physical. That's the start of a destructive cycle. The result is mental and physical weakness. You become tired from inactivity, and you become less active because you are tired. Every day that the cycle continues, you become weaker. The best and maybe only way out of that cycle is physical activity, even though you don't feel like it at all. You cannot think your way out of this cycle. If you are in that cycle, get out now; it doesn't get better on its own. Stop what you are doing immediately and use your body for something physical until it is exhausted, then get some sleep.

That's just how we work, whether we like it or not. I know that people are in the habit of telling you to get some rest. I don't think that is wrong, just often misplaced. Physical exertion is a rest from mental stress. It's a rest from poor circulation and all the other types of atrophy. We know that our bodies were evolved or designed for movement. It's not just that they are good at activity but that they require it. You are literally in a state of atrophy when you are inactive for too long. The step after atrophy is decay. Inactivity is the same as dying, and it feels like it. Run from it, literally. People have different points of view on what the appropriate amount of activity is. Well, I don't know for sure either. But I live by the rule: Put to use every part of your body daily that you plan to keep, and at least once a week, ask a bit more of the parts that you want to improve.

COMPLICATE THINGS

Recall much earlier when I pointed out that when we apply our drives to our overall experience, they seem general and broad but very strong. This is true and an important concept to understand when thinking of them in our overall psychology. But our drives themselves are biological and specific once we uncover them. They then can seem simple when explained by human evolutionary biologists. Having the knowledge of the forces influencing us below our conscious perception makes awareness of the manifestations of those forces possible. And that is a true superpower that's relatively new to us. Strangely, we haven't fully utilized this immeasurable power yet, but I'm pushing for it. We aren't entirely in control of ourselves consciously. Knowing that and knowing exactly where and how we are driven is a gift waiting to be received.

Knowledge of our biology is a gift because it is the most direct and reliable way to learn to control ourselves. Awareness of our biological motivations is a superpower because it puts our hands on the steering wheel of our trajectory. Awareness of our impulses in the moment we are stimulated affords us a choice that otherwise is impossible to see. We must know our biological tendencies to decide what to do about them. And we can do something about them if we accept that we have them. That is special.

"Between stimulus and response, there is a space. In that space is our power to choose our response. In our response lies our growth and our freedom" – Viktor Frankl via Stephen R. Covey.

This special trick of creating opportunity through impulse awareness was proven successful thousands of years ago by Stoics, some of whom literally nearly conquered the world as a result. Even though they had no specific scientific knowledge of these things, they were able to objectively observe the effect of internal forces on thoughts, behavior, and outcomes. They sought to subvert this force to seek truth and make better decisions. They described this as *apatheia*. Apatheia was considered a state a person could achieve in which they are free from the disturbances of *passions*. Passions to the Greeks were defining instinctive emotional drives of humans. Being free from the disturbances of these forces gave them the highest level of control of their reactions to what was happening. Despite the common misconception, the stoics were not seeking to eliminate emotions; rather, they created a practice to domesticate emotion to eliminate the negative influence on decisions, choices, and reactions. And it works.

We are sophisticated animals, but we are still animals. If you disagree, spend an hour watching wild animal behavior documentaries, and then sit in any informal public place and quietly observe people the same way. You'll notice that maybe we aren't as disconnected from our instincts as we like to believe. Then, turn that experience introspective. You will find that you can be interestingly complex and sophisticated, but only on purpose when you try. The rest of the time, you are a straightforward, predictable animal. Our thoughts and behaviors are sort of like breathing in that way. You can do it voluntarily or involuntarily, but in any case, you are still breathing.

If you don't believe me, consider the behavior of a human deprived of air, water, or food. We turn into destructive wild animals relatively quickly. And when we are deprived of our drives, which are less essential to survival, we experience milder biological motivations that affect our behavior and thoughts. We can think our thoughts with sophisticated intent, but if we stop acting intentionally sophisticated, we don't necessarily stop thinking and behaving. So, when we relax our critical thinking, our evolutionary default thinking is what's left to a higher degree, and it is more primal. That doesn't mean bad.

When we stop critical or higher thinking, we slip down to a state of efficiency. This isn't all bad. Brain power is expensive for our energy supplies and doesn't stimulate more energy like other ways of spending energy. Have you ever noticed that sitting in a chair and busting your brain for a few hours can exhaust you far more than doing manual labor? There is a reason for that. Brain power takes lots of energy. This is energy that we need and, in many ways, seek to preserve.

We have a default hands-free self-driving reality to some degree. It is beneficial and efficient. But Evolution doesn't update our firmware very often. So, we have a minor disagreement with ourselves. Have you ever responded to something confidently and, after thinking it through, later realized that you don't agree entirely with your response or behavior? Of course you have; we all have. That's where you can spot the disagreement between your primitive and your sophisticated self. While the disagreements may be minor, we likely spend much of our time in our more primitive state. Minor disagreements are substantial when they add up and possibly compound.

That default, more primal influence is being studied and described by brilliant people, including human evolutionary biologists, as we speak. They break down the complex reaches of our personality into small parts we can understand, such as tendencies, traits, interests, and cognitive biases. And these small parts are being used by many other - ologists such as psychologists to make meaningful descriptions of exactly how we may disagree with our sophisticated self and what we can do about it.

What do we do about all that for now? Well, we can't think critically all the time. We wouldn't want to. Critical thinking is questioning, analyzing, interpreting, and evaluating sufficiently enough to create a quality judgment, discernment, or categorization. It starts by intentionally making thoughts instead of them just popping into your head. This is best initiated by asking yourself questions and attempting to answer them. While supremely useful, that process is very demanding and, by its nature, disconnects us from the connected experience of living. It's like watching game tape instead of playing a game. Or like evaluating your dance moves instead of just dancing. It is vital to spend time in the flow of things, present, and aware of the feelings and experiences. Human connections are best made in that flow.

Meanwhile, we cannot avoid critical thinking and expect to improve. So, we must decide when it's best to spend our precious brain power and take the wheel. I propose that everyone maintains a sustained practice in critical thinking development and mindfulness. You can grow your power and ability with these skills by practicing them. Plan on thirty to sixty minutes a couple of days a week or more for critical thinking.

A practice of critical thinking I mentioned that is also useful for staying informed is to listen to or read an intellectual debate of opposing views to something relevant or interesting to you and use reason to write out the logical positions or arguments. Try to create a quality logical question and answer it. Then, edit it. Inspecting for logical consistency has nothing to do with your opinion, feelings, or judgments. It's more like grammatical math. Often, people equate logic with something that makes sense to them and equate reason with information that they like. Those equivocations are dangerous and will more likely reflect a bias or unreasonable emotion instead of the truth.

Incorrect logic leads to false conclusions. The fewer false conclusions you have, the more successful you can be. Incorrect logic is caused by logically invalid reasoning, which is called a logical fallacy. Reason and logic are tools for you to inspect what things really are instead of what you want them to be. I'm not suggesting that you must become an expert logician, but having a working knowledge of the basics is profoundly useful. At the very least, learn the most common logical fallacies and practice spotting them. This practice will help you become aware of when you are making the same mistake later and save you from relying on false conclusions. That is the same as operating with better information.

When you are proficient and always recently familiar with thinking critically, you can fire it like a pistol on your hip when you need to. Just like a pistol, you don't want to fire off your big brain at everything. Also, just like a pistol, it doesn't do you any good if you leave it at home or it doesn't function properly. So, when to fire it outside of regular practice is the question. One could make a good argument that this is the very essence of free will.

Deciding when to pull out your big brain and fire off critical thinking requires sustained awareness and identified targets. One of these targets should be when you feel strong emotions rising that are calling you to action or expression. That is a great indicator to pull your weapon. Step away from the situation, take cover, clear your mind, and then think as hard as possible. You will immediately notice a few things.

First, you will not want to disengage from the interaction and start thinking rationally. You will have a strong desire to stay irrationally engaged. Disengage anyway; you now know you will perform more like a pissed-off primate. That is precisely what you should be suspicious of. We all know damn well that we have it in us to bite someone's face off and tear their limbs apart like a chimp. Whether we do it literally, to their emotions, or to their reputation, we do it just the same. If you are going to make that kind of attack, you would first want to think it all the way through to be effective anyhow. You will relinquish all power and act counterproductively or destructively to your own cause if you react emotionally.

Second, you will notice that when you do try, it is difficult to think while you are fired up. You will have to suppress your emotions and gain composure to engage your critical thinking. Use the meditation and mindfulness skills that you have been practicing. Lastly, you will notice a divide between what was causing your emotions and the content of the interaction. You will notice that serving your emotions and serving your cause are in disagreement. You will understand what is happening to you and how it's different from what you may want. Ask yourself what you want the result to be and why. Then, you can reengage the situation. You will know exactly what to do and be able to execute it calmly and powerfully, even if it is best to concede.

"The best answer to anger is silence." Marcus Aurelius

This is the most overall impactful skill a person can have. It is mechanistically simple to understand and execute. It is only difficult emotionally. You can handle that. This skill will change your overall results so quickly and intensely that it will seem incomprehensible. You can benefit from this practice even if you think you are already pretty good at it. If you have any room to improve this skill, take advantage of it. The slightest incremental improvement in your performance at this most impactful time will be a significant gain. I have never met anyone, including myself, who doesn't have room to improve on taming themselves when they are fired up. In other words, it's a game changer.

I didn't designate this to only negative emotions that come in too hot. Positive ones do as well, and they are equally dangerous. But all we are focusing on here are the feelings that call you to action or expression. That is our identified target for using critical thinking. If you have an overwhelming positive emotion, enjoy it. If you start to do something about it, that is when you stop and think first. Draw your thought weapon. Doing this with strong positive and negative emotions will take practice. You can quickly forget that you are trying to do things differently.

Another essential time to use your critical thinking is anytime you can identify that someone is trying to persuade you. We all make the mistake of underestimating the power of persuasion and believe we are steadfast and make up our own minds. Well, that may be true, but only when our critical thinking is engaged. Persuasion is remarkably powerful, especially when it is received by a person in a primitive or emotional state. A good rhetorician can change anyone's mind for them without them even realizing it. We need to protect ourselves from this, especially now that anyone can use language-trained artificial intelligence to make impeccable persuasive arguments and deliver them directly to you via the internet. If you own a smartphone, you have manipulative agents in your pocket, bedroom, and maybe even the toilet.

How do you tell when persuasion is being used on you? The best way is to ask yourself, "What's the motivation?" Just focusing your attention on trying to uncover the motivation will insulate you from persuasion even if you never discover it. A reasonable level of cynicism and skepticism is a shield from being misled or duped. If the motivation is to get you to do something or believe something, it is clearly persuasion. Ask yourself, am I being convinced to do something or believe something? However, a good rhetorician can hide their motivation very well and often not present it until after they have already hooked you by making you feel something. If you catch yourself being moved to fear, compassion, sympathy, arousal, or any other emotion by someone, be suspicious if you are enticed to take an action or adopt a belief. That's the time to critically evaluate what is going on, challenge the argument, and make a judgment for yourself.

Persuasion isn't intrinsically sinister; it is an important and normal part of our communication. The motivation behind it can be honorable, such as your friend trying to persuade you to do something they believe you will both have fun doing together. A pitch to get you to take a day off and go to the beach with your friend is great, and you want people with good intentions who are motivated to persuade you. So, another way to spot persuasion that needs your powerful brain is the source. If someone doesn't know you but it feels like they do when they are convincing you of something, be critical and skeptical.

Here are some ways to spot persuasive communication by looking at the communication itself. Look to see if it includes:

1. A claim of some kind, such as "Palestinians have a legitimate right to the land of Israel and Jerusalem."
2. Repetition. Are the points being emphasized by being repeated?
3. Colloquial or simple language. Such as, "The idiots supporting Palestine don't have a brain in their head; you get me?" This is used to connect with you as if they are a friend you have been talking to for years, and it has a weird way of instilling trust.
4. Jargon words. Is there technical terminology meant to make them seem smarter than you? Example - The Israel occupation is comprised of colonial oppressors with power-thirsty Machiavellian intentions.
5. Emotive appeals. Is there descriptive language that is meant to make you feel something such as terrible pain,

overwhelming joy, or unbelievably awful?
6. Inclusive language. Look for the word "we" from a stranger.
7. Rhetorical questions. Such as "Should we allow this?"
8. Bias. This is noticeable when an opposing idea isn't brought up or considered at all. Usually, it is so because the speaker has a reason to prefer their perspective more than searching for the truth. Example – "Palestinian children are being killed, and it must be stopped." While in this example, that claim isn't untrue or immoral, it doesn't account for the Israeli perspective that Jewish children are being killed and held hostage at the same time.

You can learn to spot persuasion in many more ways, but these are usually more than enough. Now, what to do about it? How do you use your critical thinking when you spot persuasion of suspect intent? The most efficient way is to challenge the whole thing from a different point of view. If you really like the argument for something, stop for a second and create a great opposing argument. For example, if the claim is "Palestine is fighting for their freedom from oppression by Israel.", make an opposite argument that Israel is defending its freedom from Palestine. You will unveil the strengths and weaknesses of the claim or learn what additional information is needed. Then, see which argument you like better. Even if you still like the argument more than the argument against it, you will know that it holds up well to your own criticism. You can be more sure of yourself, so to speak.

The only persuasive argument you should ever repeat to another person is one that holds up to quality criticism. And it will only be as strong as your ability to criticize it.

Come up with some way to monitor progress that works for you. One way to monitor progress also happens to be the next good place to use your critical thinking skills. Reflective journaling is remarkably powerful but simple. At the end of each day, skim over the previous day's entry. Then, reflect on the day you just completed. Critically and honestly, think about what you did and didn't do. Think about how you felt and in what context, etc. Write about it a bit. Take a measurement of how well you did at an initiative you made for yourself, such as how many times you primitively responded to something and how many times you responded sophisticatedly. For example:

"Today, I was upset and responded primitively. I said things that were unfairly harsh. They were neither necessary nor completely true, and I'm sure it won't help my relationship. I also shared a provocative post that I can't verify its accuracy. I'll bet I was propagating a bias that I hold; I better investigate that. I can do better. On the other hand, my boss was pissing me off, but I handled it well. I calmed myself before responding and suspected that he was trying to bait me into an unnecessary conflict that would yield poor results. So, I calmly but assertively requested to delay the conversation until after lunch. He was much more amicable by then. He even apologized for being an ass while I gave him my full present attention. He seemed to grow more vulnerable as I listened to him instead of arguing."

Then, write a couple of goals or initiatives you know you could accomplish tomorrow. You don't have to put a load of energy and eloquence into this. Then sleep on it. Although seemingly small, this practice will move mountains in your mind and subsequently in your life.

Those are my suggested targets where I know critical thinking power will be effectively and efficiently used for you. Other identified targets and applications that fit your situation specifically need to be created and discovered for yourself. Your assignment now is to pull out that big brain and think through when you believe it would be a good time to detach and switch from the default primal state to a sophisticated critical thinker and why. A quality strategy is to seek to reduce failures and increase victories. So, a two-part strategy with two kinds of targets. Target type one is to identify what is screwing things up for me, and target type two is what is working for me.

One good place to look for targets that are causing problems is to look back at the time right before things usually go wrong for you. What reliable indicators are there in the hour before I fight with my spouse or friend, decide to go to the bar, eat loads of shitty food, start procrastinating, feel lazy, become irritable, make a poor decision at work, etc.? Look back at that hour and lay everything out. What were you doing, and why were you doing it? What feelings did you have? Who were you around, and what were the conditions? Be curious as to how these things may have led you to fail yourself. Look for patterns and break them as soon as you recognize them next time. Break them with critical thinking. Evaluate what the conditions are versus what they could be if you changed them. Consider the possible results and make judgments about them. This quality self-evaluation will prevent you from justifying poor behavior to yourself.

Do the same thing for the hour before things go right for you. Except this time, try to repeat the things you were doing, thinking, and feeling right before something worked really well for you. Repeat patterns that lead you to please a friend, arouse a partner, accomplish something meaningful, impress a colleague, and feel inspired! Maybe you will figure out why these things affect you, and maybe you won't. But either way, you can use them as a tool just by knowing they do affect you and by eliminating or repeating the patterns.

Write out your plan of when to think critically as completely as you can, go back and organize it, and edit it until it is the best you can make it. That whole process is important. If you only give it a few minutes of effortless thought, you are performing something like a chimpanzee, wondering what it would be like to be something special. If you don't find a way to hang on to your knowledge and intentions, they will soon disappear from your mind forever as you slip back to a more primitive state of efficiency, and you may never notice they are gone. You have no idea what incredible things you have already forgotten because they are forgotten. Let that strange logical fact settle in and motivate you to keep better notes.

We have a strong impulse to simplify and categorize things in our experience. This is a drive we need to understand to examine drives in general. You may have heard this expressed as "putting things in a box." For example, when we think of something in simple terms, such as a rock, we usually think of the most typical characterizations of a rock. We may think of something that fits in our hand that is hard, heavy, opaque, and mildly misshapen. But we know a crystal-clear diamond is a rock, and so is a giant boulder, flowing lava, sand blowing in the wind, the glass in your window, or holding your wine. But we put a simplified label on it. Then, we think about things mostly within the limitations of that box and label. That is fantastic for going through every day and conceptualizing the many things around us with a sense of control that helps us navigate living. If we spent all day classifying and eloquently describing every type of rock and everything else around us, we wouldn't be able to function. However, nothing fits in a box or is confined to the limits of a label, and nothing is disconnected from everything else.

So, you can't ever close a box. Any amount of description inflicts an equal or greater amount of limitation. When we do this to ourselves, it inherits a risk of becoming a limiting belief that restricts us in some way. We want to be able to be a diamond, lava, boulder, and blowing sand, not just a rock. We must instead challenge our assumptions with curiosity as to what is possible.

For example, sex drive is a very strong drive in humans. It gets allocated a high level of our energy. And we can sense it everywhere inside our mind, body, and environment. Yet, it's often reduced to a few specific turn-ons and an easy way to satisfy. For example, engaging in your favorite pornographic video category or erotic literature. Or a repetitive sexual routine with a partner that doesn't have a prelude or seductive period beforehand. The easy, quick ways are the least resistant paths to releasing this energy. This is also the best way to not use this energy for much at all. It is a tidy little box with a few labels that you must empty regularly. Or a person's sex drive can be simplified and stuffed in a box of all the turn-offs or ways one is trying to suppress this drive for one reason or another.

The suppression box is also hazardous because it gets filled but doesn't get emptied. It will burst, and the energy can uncontrollably go into many parts of one's life. This could be when we see sexual energy sometimes fueling conflict—conflict with ourselves, other people, and our environment. This is probably akin to what we call *sexual frustration*. Destructive conflict is the most damaging and unnecessary thing humans have ever thought up. It's the boogieman in the flesh. So, it's worth avoiding intentionally to be successful.

The definitions I use in interpersonal relationships to ensure my intentions are honorable and successful are as follows: <u>Confrontation</u> is the willingness to address something difficult that may be received poorly. That is productive, especially when followed by negotiation. <u>Negotiation</u> is a discussion attempting to reach an agreement. However, when we confront but don't seek an agreement, it's tyranny or conflict. For me, <u>Conflict</u> is the desire to engage in some form of fighting in an attempt to validate one's own position of incompatibility by defeating opposition through force, manipulation, or exclusionary tactics. It is possible to not reach an agreement and still avoid conflict. That's why we use the trick of agreeing to disagree. That shouldn't be used as an insult or exclusionary tactic but rather an agreement to hold our overall relationship and mutual respect in much higher regard than a single difference in opinion.

It is necessary for your success to have people around you that think differently than you. Conflict is usually destructive, especially with a bit of extra sexual energy, frustration, or irritability. There is somewhere between a place of over-deprivation and overindulgence that is the most productive for our sexuality. The East would call this balance.

Sex drive is excellent for making love. I adore the expression making love. It points to the fact that we can channel our sex drive as a motivator to engage in and experience all the things that create the conditions for love in a relationship that may lead to sex. Or sex drive can push us to become healthy, hygienic, accomplished, articulate, interesting, or whatever traits we believe increase our desirability to get into an intimate relationship. Those are both great things for us, and sex is a strong motivator.

Sex drive is also great for making inspiration, art, progressing through struggle, making visions, and making laughter and excitement. It can make experiences more sensual and connected with the environment and yourself. Sex energy can be harnessed to have more available energy for living. There is no limit to where you can direct the positive energy of your sex drive. It is strong; use it. Many great athletes, artists, and leaders have claimed to have used their sex drive intentionally to improve their abilities, such as Floyd Mayweather, Nikola Tesla, Isaac Newton, Beethoven, Leonardo Da Vinci, and Henry Thoreau.

Those are all men who have claimed a marked and noticeable short-term benefit of preserving their sexual energy. This isn't evidence that it doesn't work for women also, but instead, it probably describes the difference in how this energy is built up and released between the genders. I'm not making a scientific proposition. I'm pointing out these anecdotal observations to help you critically think about how you function. There is no wrong answer here other than the one that isn't accurate in your evaluation of yourself.

I don't know of any uber-successful women in the West claiming to channel this energy, but I'm confident some exist. I do know of a significant movement of Western women joining long-standing Ayurvedic (eastern holistic) practices such as yoga, tantra, mindfulness, and ceremony to "create healing." And the path to the "divine feminine" depends very much on getting familiar with and enhancing feminine sexual energy. Ayurveda has specific advice about how and when to practice abstinence to channel sexual energy into pursuits of mental and physical development as well as many other pursuits in sexuality.

For some, it is a simple method of just abstaining from sexual release a day before doing something important. For others, it seems best to engage in a limited amount of additional sensual or erotic thoughts or behavior before doing something creative. One interesting way from tantric practices that isn't practiced much in the West is engaging in sexual or sensual activity but avoiding orgasm, or at least not making it the motivation. The motivation instead is to enhance and use this energy as the way to a deeply connected state of experience and existence.

Remember, our aim is to cultivate our drives to work for us. In my opinion, outside of reproduction, our culture hasn't figured out a productive use for our sex drive other than using it to sell things and cause problems. We especially mess it up regularly in relationships. I'm not confident I have any authority to suggest the proper ways to use it culturally. But I can say with certainty that when we demonize sex drive and create a repressive and shameful framework for thinking about it, we fail terribly. We need to challenge our assumptions with curiosity, as I'm doing here. We need to understand this instilled shame and evaluate its impact for ourselves. On the other hand, losing control of desire can lead to dangerous excess hedonism. There is a balance and proper orientation for our sex drive that each of us can find.

I don't have the answers to the difficult specific questions of how we should deal with what is appropriate in regard to intimacy. I do know that there are lots of questions and ideas from governments, religions, science, parents, and cultural law for how we should deal with our sex drive and consequential actions. It impacts our evolution by being selection-driven, and it affects our regular thinking to adopt sexual strategy. There are also other considerations of consent, disease, pregnancy, abortion, custody, etc. It's tough to suggest we know what is best, but I do know that lying to ourselves and others when we feel ashamed of our sex drive is a catastrophe and prevents us from taking responsibility. With honesty and responsibility, we are always more enabled to do good.

There may be some good information to learn from Tantra on how to cultivate our sex drive to work for our cause. Tantra is an ancient eastern practice thousands of years in the making. The word in Sanskrit means something like weaving or composing, and the tantric practices have become a way to incorporate the physical and spiritual life together. The general idea is to practice intimacy in a meditative and spiritual way to increase sexual energy, purity, and connectedness instead of seeking orgasmic pleasure exclusively. This is done because it is believed to have utility in spiritual enlightenment and in life. That is very different than just having a goal of getting off. It illustrates well the efficacy of harnessing our vital sexual energy for other useful things besides orgasm and making babies, such as healing, connectedness, self-acceptance, and enlightenment.

Tantra's prominent contribution, even in its early beginnings, is its attempt to transform people through our bodies instead of despite our bodies. Using our bodies is something we are good at and can be effective with. That is precisely what we are doing by cultivating our drives. Transcending our bodies to improve somehow will never work for humans. We aren't separate from our bodies after all. Instead, we regress to adopting shaming, repression, and deceit when we feel disconnected from who and what we are.

It seems to me that sex is another place where we don't have a good platform for dealing with a strong biological drive, so my suggestion is going to sound conservative. But it's really more of a cautious, practical approach than a conservative one. I have experience with monogamy and polyamory. A simple, practical observation I can share with you is that monogamy is difficult enough yet the easiest to be successful with and efficient. A monogamous relationship will leave you time and energy to focus on other things more than other types of intimate relationship endeavors. It is also more deeply fulfilling because it is focused and unfragmented.

Nothing will distract you from your vision faster than relationship issues. It's not worth increasing the prevalence of relationship woes. Polyamory involves more than two people in one relationship. Relationships are an extremely complicated ongoing negotiation with sensitive emotions involved. That is difficult enough for two people, and every person you add compounds the complexity and likelihood of failure. Even if it is successful, it will require significantly more effort that you could have been spending on other worthwhile endeavors and limited or no additional benefit.

I suggest working very diligently to get in and stay in an intimate relationship with someone. Then, go after continually revitalizing and sustaining an intimate vibe between you. Seduce your partner unabashedly regularly. Encourage and reward them for doing so for you. Try to keep your partner as the subject of your fantasizing. Make it novel and tell them about it. Talk about sex with them at times when you cannot follow through with the act. Let there be some healthy periods of privation between you to build up energy. Strike a balance and have spontaneity. That's more than enough fun and pleasure a person should seek, and it's in the productive spirit of unity that is very real and deeply meaningful.

Now that our drives are working for us and are turned on in this new life, we will want strength and commitment.

SELF-DISCIPLINE (P.D.R.)

In my opinion, the combination of the words self and discipline is confusing in our language evolution because we don't have a better way to say what we mean. This impediment may be dissuading our culture from using this incredibly powerful and transformative ability. When we use the word self-discipline properly, I think we are talking about the explicit act of a person to improve himself through intentional and sustained implementation of challenging methods and routines. But, discipline's definition is training people to obey rules or a code of behavior, using punishment to correct disobedience. Why would anyone want to apply that to themselves? They wouldn't unless they lived in an extreme ideology that made them believe that they were a useless sinner who could only find salvation through punishing the evil out of themselves or something of low self-respect like that. We know for sure that won't work. The result that will likely come from self-punishment is self-resentment or worse.

If we look up the two words as hyphenated, self-discipline, we can find one accepted definition that gets closer: Correction or regulation of oneself for the sake of improvement. It's still no good. We can't just have a definition that has a relevant opposing definition still in use. Or it is confusing because we are to understand that discipline means something different if we apply it to ourselves instead of someone else, but only sometimes. Also, this definition still has "correction," suggesting self-punishment. Positive punishment only works when you can't escape it or stop it. Staying motivated to punish yourself isn't the best possible way to improve.

We may think we don't like the thing we call self-discipline. We are wrong about that, and we can change it. So, let's start by changing our understanding to be more accurate to what we want to accomplish. I may be wrong, but I don't think we have a better word for self-discipline. So, I'll suggest a phrase that I came up with. I call it persistent developmental resolve, or PDR for short.

PDR is the explicit act of improving oneself through the intentional and sustained implementation of challenging methods and routines. It is persistent and requires resolve to complete methods and routines that are difficult and uncomfortable as well as ones that are simple and pleasurable. Okay, we can work with that for sure. Let's start with what it means to improve oneself. To begin with, it feels terrific and meaningful, especially for your self-worth and confidence. Improving yourself is also a profound process that creates fertile ground for happiness to arise. If you are improving yourself intentionally, you have created a larger vision of yourself. You have also been honest and humbled yourself to discover where you can improve. You have encouraged yourself as the father or mother of that vision, so to speak. You have decided that you are qualified to judge and measure your progress.

Take a close look at the person that the improvement process creates. This person is a supreme visionary, honest and humble, deeply encouraging, the most powerful authority for approval, and a person of action. You become this to yourself and the world. From this type of person, happiness, success, and inspiration are regular occurrences. Notice it isn't even the object of what is improving that makes the magic happen for you; it is you, the subject of the process, that always benefits. In other words, you can improve any seemingly insignificant thing about yourself for the better and make enormously significant changes for yourself overall. The process of self-improvement is also a parallel process that leads to developing or realizing your conscientiousness, which is a primary indicator of success. You can't put a price on how valuable it is to your psyche to take on a challenge to improve, no matter how small, and see it through to victory. You get to feel your worthiness and learn to trust yourself enough to rely on yourself.

Improving yourself is not the same as improving your status.

Rise in status is often a result of improving yourself, but that is only true because people who are very good at improving themselves will likely find ways to be more successful. This is easier when you have the skill set to be competent at almost anything. Notice it's the PDR they are good at, not one thing, and they can use it very efficiently on many things. It isn't a one-and-done deal. The whole of everything is constantly developing and changing. Even if you applied remarkable PDR to the stock market, for example, and made a load of money, your information and strategy would quickly antiquate because the market's conditions always change. You will lose your gains if you drop your PDR and continue to place bets based on old information. It would be best if you continued improving your information and adjusting your strategy persistently. This means you would need to be developing your position constantly. You need to be strongly proficient at the skill PDR for every day of your life. This is where the "intentional and <u>sustained</u>" part of the definition comes in.

Having strong Persistent Developmental Resolve, previously known as self-discipline, is more special than it seems at first impression. We understand that it can bring us useful and desired improvement, but that isn't all it does. Joe Rogan points out the essential nature of PDR, saying things such as, *It's the only way we have available to realize any potential in anything. There isn't another way and that you have to show up even when you don't want to. Showing up is like 90 percent of it.* He shows that motivation isn't the way; it's a starting line to a marathon at best. Alan Watts described PDR as *"…the way people bring heaven to earth… It's connecting the mystical with the practical.… You can bring higher visions to life. Discipline grounds the experience of self-realization and brings it to life.… There is no pleasure in this world without skill.… Mastery of some technique is required to represent and carry through the vision."*

Let's get hands-on with improving and using PDR. First, decide your state of malleability. How easily do you allow change? Be honest with yourself; there is no wrong answer except the one that will stop you from being effective. Are you as set in your ways as steel or shapeable as sand? Or are you somewhere in the middle? Figuring out your tendency to allow change in yourself will help you create an expectation and measure your progress. Being aware of your malleability also gives you the power to adjust it. Notice and evaluate your general disposition. Are you looking and listening for new useful information to discover? Or are you only paying attention to things that confirm what you already know? You can choose between these perspectives. In fact, you are the only one who can change this about you.

To improve the skill of changing more easily, spend some time doing something new that's uncomfortable, such as eating a new food. Also, try listening to something that you disagree with. You don't have to like the new. You must practice being open, honest, and fair. Those are the skills for a proper disposition to achieve good discovery.

On the contrary, if you tend to change too easily and adopt every new idea, you could practice being more rigid. New ideas are exciting and can be amazing breakthroughs, but more often, they are failures. That is the nature of progression. New is also unverified, unreliable, and has a higher risk. A good way to practice controlling an over-attraction to novelty is to ask critical questions about new things in comparison to reliable things. For example, when you hear about the next new amazing diet, try being adequately critical of the specific claims. Ask yourself, where does the evidence adequately prove that I will be healthier and better looking? Then, steel man the argument. That is to try to create a quick argument about why it isn't a good diet. Now, you have two perspectives to consider in making a balanced decision. You are considering what can go right and what can go wrong.

These practices will start positioning you to persistently develop yourself. But as I mentioned earlier, the most important skill to develop is to take proper action even when you don't feel like it. How do you regularly do something even when you don't feel like doing it?

First, you can't do anything regularly if you are randomly thinking up things to improve and change about yourself and then give them a higher priority than your previous ideas because they are new and exciting. This is a lack of direction and will manifest your unconscientiousness. If you have created a plan for your vision and a schedule with a routine, then the thing you may not feel like doing is already more important to you than it would have been if you had no plan. You probably really like your improved vision of yourself that you know is on the other side of your plan. So, you are part of the way to defeating not feeling like doing it. Even if the alternative action you are being seduced by is nothing or relaxation, it is still a thing you'd rather be doing. Refer back to the "Love and Struggle" chapter at the beginning of this text. Often, you are being successfully seduced away from your plan and into an alternative that is more pleasing for the moment. It is because your plan involves some struggle, and you haven't fallen in love with it yet. While you are working on that, there are a few methods to help.

Write down what you'd rather be doing. Keep it as a reward for doing what you should be doing. This only takes a second. Change your thought structure away from thinking, *I could do what I want that will please me now instead of what I want most for my life and take an empty, unearned award now.* And change it to; *I could do what I want most for my life and reward myself with what I want to please myself with right after.* This eliminates the effort and pain of making a sacrifice. Let's say your calendar alarm said it's time to go to the gym, and you'd rather eat pizza in front of the TV. Say to yourself, "I am going to go to the gym, and then I'll eat pizza in front of the TV, and I will have earned it." Change this thought structure often enough, and you will change your thought pattern to something much more profound. You will soon have the strength to make the desired change you once called a sacrifice. Sacrifice will eventually start becoming a positive indicator for you that doesn't dissuade you.

There is nothing wrong with <u>rewarding</u> yourself. Any kind of positive reinforcement for getting it done is good. You don't have to be incredible at everything every time you do it. Doing the right thing poorly still keeps you moving toward your vision tremendously more than doing the wrong thing. You will gain more and feel better by performing poorly rather than quitting.

The magic of using this method is that you will quickly find that if you can bribe yourself into just getting started when you feel like shit, getting started will cure feeling like shit. In our example, you will likely get a charge from the gym and may forget about the pizza and TV. Or at least you will enjoy it guilt-free, preserving your self-worth. The gym example is an easy one to spot, but this trick can be used for all things on your calendar, big and small. If you don't feel like doing something on your plan, ask yourself why and discover what you'd rather do. Use the alternative as a reward to keep you on track to your next remarkable destination.

Another method is to use <u>mirror talk</u>. Stand in front of the mirror when you don't feel like doing something. Clear your mind for a minute, re-experience your bigger vision of yourself, look yourself in the eyes, and ask, "What do I truly want to do most?" Then, wait while keeping eye contact. Wait for it. You may be surprised to find this the most effective method for you. See for yourself.

Another method is <u>thought destruction</u>. Be aware of when you start thinking of flaking out on your plan. Since you now have a calendar with all your plans and intentions on it, it's easy to spot when you aren't doing the thing you meant to be doing. Examine those thoughts of flaking briefly, notice they are trash, and throw them away. Carry on with your plans as if they are sacred, not to be rethought or rewritten. Just do the damn thing you said you would, and don't ask questions. You aren't required to feel like doing anything in the plan anyway; you just need to do them. You made yourself a promise, and that's all you need to consider. Keeping your commitment to yourself is itself the essential transformative substrate for the fruits of your desire.

Pick the methods that work for you and create some of your own if you need to. You won't need them for long. Your mind and body will adapt, and old ways will fade away quickly if you stay consistent with correcting course. You will get stronger. Now, let's clear up what stronger means and why it's essential.

Strength is the ability to withstand. It's often confused with power, which is the ability to impose. You use power to impose force on something; your strength enables you to withstand the consequences of that force. If you wield power without adequate strength, you will be injured or destroyed in some way. Any human can lift something heavier than they can withstand but will slip a disk, pull muscles, and tear tendons. The effect of lifting more than you can withstand in your life can injure your psyche. Having sufficient strength of mind, body, and character to withstand your tremendous power is the fundamental path to complete success in life. What matters most to the strength of your success is based on <u>how</u> you accomplish it, not <u>if</u> you do. Weak success dies easily. It is vulnerable.

Power is relatively easy to come by, and there are a lot of books about how to get it. Most show us the shortcuts to power. I urge you to build your strength instead, and the best kinds of power follow on their own. Strength comes from overcoming yourself and facing challenges. Muster the courage to face difficult and uncomfortable things and trust you will adapt. *"It's not about how hard you can hit; it's about how hard you can get hit and keep moving forward"* (Rocky Balboa). Persistent developmental resolve or self-discipline is the best process to build strength. While it isn't as fast as usurping power from somewhere to get what you want, strength is better, sustainable, and required for true power. Also, it doesn't take very long to get strong in character once you are consistent. It's in your true nature. Or, if you prefer science, strength is written in your genetic code, waiting to be activated.

The truth is you will become strong or get destroyed. You don't get a third choice. You will get tested and injured many times and be presented with the only option you have in this regard. Do I become stronger or get destroyed? If you feel like a victim, you are injured. You need strength urgently to start feeling like a survivor. If you are alive and reading this, it is impossible that you are a victim instead of a survivor. Victims are dead. Survivors are alive. Yes, people do get victimized, but the moment it's over, the responsibility to recover falls completely on the shoulders of the person who was victimized. I know that isn't easy or fair, but that truth is necessary to face. No matter how terrible your current situation may be, if you are alive, you have something important to contribute that the world needs, and we are counting on you to find the courage to build strength enough to do it. Even more importantly, you are counting on you.

If you are living in good circumstances and doing well, finding strength is also critical. It's a much better experience to strengthen yourself intentionally instead of waiting for life to step on you to see if you can survive. Everyone experiences devastating events in their lives, maybe even multiple times. You may have experienced this at least once; if you haven't, you will. That is how our system is built. This is life.

You should accept this challenging part of our fate as the challenge to be prepared for and grow from. Otherwise, success may disappear the moment you get crushed under a difficult test. Basically, having good PDR makes you accustomed to and adept at dealing with struggle, turning it into success. So, when life throws you a tragic struggle, you won't have to suffer as much, even though you may be in the presence of pain. That experience will be familiar to you, and you will have learned many times over how to deal with painful struggles while turning them into success. You now know that the function of struggles that befall you is to strengthen and grow you. They are the stones on the path to greater success.

"The impediment to action advances action, what stands in the way becomes the way." – Marcus Aurelius.

With strong PDR you will be optimistic, steady, and ready to overcome. Consider how pointless it is to measure your gains when you are susceptible to losing them all with one tragic blow. Furthermore, if you are strong, you will have the skill and presence of mind to help those less prepared and weak when tragedy strikes. That is the greatest success there is. That describes heroes and heroines.

Strength is also your protection from unwanted distraction and seduction. It is very easy to get pulled off course and persuaded. There are plenty of destructive negative paths all around you that can be quite seductive, such as power itself, dramatic ideologies, destructive dogmas, nihilistic subcultures, hedonistic party groups, drugs, etc. Most of us don't observe this about ourselves and have seriously overestimated our ability to remain cognizant. You can't afford only to believe you are strong because seductive distraction is a sleight of hand. Belief cannot protect you when the truth is hidden. Seduction doesn't cut you; it convinces you to cut yourself. I've done it. It doesn't matter how strong you believe you are when you are under attack from yourself. You must be strong to your unconscious depths. PDR instills more of this kind of strength every day.

Suffering is a choice for those who are strong but inevitable for the weak.

Pain is a sensation. Agony is continual pain. Suffering is when we abstract pain and agony away from the source and into our psyche. Pain hurts, but agony can break you, meaning it can defeat your strength and ability to withstand the pressure of pain from flooding into how you feel about everything. Just like a dam breaking will flood a river basin and wash away everything beautiful, your will has a breaking point. Having good PDR is maintaining your dam and placing new blocks all the time to build it bigger and stronger. Optimism is the mortar that holds those blocks together.

You can and should develop your resistance to suffering. Voluntarily subject yourself to uninjurious pain such as cold-water immersion. Your mind and body react and adapt to become better at experiencing pain. This increases your resistance to suffering and recalibrates your general sensitivity scale. This mental muscle for resilience to painful stimuli proves to be useful for all types of pain. Getting good at feeling a little pain is not only possible but surprisingly useful. In wrestling, we called this "pain training".

The simple idea of that was to get us used to pain so we would not be distracted by it during a match. My favorite practice was walking barefoot in the cold wet snow before training at 4:30 a.m. Back then, I was focused on not reacting to the pain, which was very intense. Many years later, I learned that I was mirroring an ancient spiritual practice found in several cultures, such as the Japanese Takigyo, where Buddhist monks meditate under a freezing waterfall.

The skill of experiencing pain as only a sensation and learning not to let it become suffering is something that happens inside of you. And everyone seems to possess the aptitude to become very proficient at it. That means you don't need to learn any complicated prerequisite skills. Just start voluntarily experiencing pain, and you will instinctively get better at it. When you do, you carry that strength with you all day. Also, it makes everything that happens the rest of the day feel better and more manageable.

First use your meditation skills to quiet your mind and focus on your intention to experience the cold water as a sensation and only a sensation. Try not to let that sensation abstract into your psychology as thoughts and feelings that will become suffering. Know that it will be a very strong sensation, but that is all it is required to be. Then, get into a cold shower or ice bath between 40 and 60 degrees Fahrenheit. Work your way down in temp over time as you adapt. Make sure your face gets wet right away; it helps slow your heart rate a bit. Don't let yourself make thoughts and feelings before getting in or while in the cold. Make the decision beforehand, and don't question it again; just do it.

Immediately, your body and mind will respond by making you feel very strongly motivated to escape the cold. All you must do is stay in it. Focus your attention on your breathing, which will be labored. Don't try to block the sensation; instead, face it and give it your full attention, then let it flow through you freely. Thirty seconds is enough to start, but try to stay longer tomorrow. But three to five minutes is best. Anything over five minutes may become dangerous. Soon, you will be able to calmly get into the cold, painful water and simply observe the sensation flowing through you non-reactively. It will no longer bother you a bit, and you will look forward to the victory of facing it, which is facing yourself.

Do this or something like this at the beginning of every day, and you will be amazed by the results. To be clear, you will never feel like doing this, and your body won't be conditioned to perceive cold water immersion as a positive sensation or reward. That's the point. Getting in the water requires courage every single time. You will try and talk yourself out of it. That is the very battle you are looking for. If you do get comfortable with it, make it colder. It's impossible to measure how beneficial it is to start every day with a victory over oneself and to have the strength to stop pain from becoming suffering. If you persist in your developmental resolve, you will find that every day, you will get better at it and get stronger. And you will carry that strength into all other aspects of life. This strength of body and mind will allow you to be much more optimistic.

Optimism is the most powerful and underrated force in humanity for success. It is also the antithesis of suffering, as well as entropy, anxiety, fear, and uncertainty. It is the way we make our environment friendly. Optimism is also a sustainable state of being that fosters our feelings of happiness, peace, and inspiration. I believe it is the most powerful force in humanity because we live in an environment that will not only try to destroy us but, conversely, will always provide the optimum conditions available to survive and thrive.

Living in our sanitized survival systems can give us the illusion that we are exempt from evolutionary pressure. But we are not. It is persistent in every moment of our lives. Notice that if you were to give up and lie motionless on the ground anywhere in the world, it wouldn't take long for the environment to gain the upper hand, and you would start dying. You will very quickly need something: water, warmth, food, and protection from other organisms. If you are missing only one or two of these things, your immune system will weaken, and you will be under attack from the microorganisms already inside and outside you.

People die from exposure. But, if you apply effort to do something about it, you can be successful at living. If we take care of each other, it's even easier. This fundamental principle is true with all aspects of our lives, no matter how abstract and complicated they are. We cannot lie down and give up on ourselves and others, or we will be destroyed. But with a little bit of effort, things turn around surprisingly quickly. There are always options. It's always only a matter of finding the good ones. Optimism is the method by which we extract the optimum conditions. It is the knowing that optimum conditions are available and looking for them. This is success.

George Bernard Shaw said it well:

"People are always blaming their circumstances for what they are. I don't believe in circumstances. The people who get on in this world are the people who get up and look for the circumstances they want and if they can't find them, make them".

Optimism has certain qualities about it that are quite dignified. You can and should choose to be optimistic, but you can't fake it, or it doesn't work. Your level of optimism can only sustain an intensity equitable to your ability to use it in the near future. So, the more competent you become, the more genuine optimism you can carry. Have faith in yourself and what you can become to make you more optimistic about the goings-on around you. Don't leave the faith to any particular god's plan alone if you do that kind of thing. Whatever creation dogma you like, it no doubt includes the fact that we are able to do good works of some sort. That's what we all agree we can do, and we can do that for sure. Let's be grateful and honor that first.

Do you see where I'm going with this yet? Good PDR or self-discipline also makes you able to be genuinely more optimistic every day you do it. This is the same as having less anxiety and fear and having more happiness and inspiration to be successful. So, while growing strong, focus on being as genuinely optimistic as possible. Value that state more than any other.

An obstacle to optimism is fear. It's difficult to feel optimistic if you are afraid. They seem to be mutually exclusive states of being. In other words, when fear creeps in, it pushes optimism out. They occupy the same space as the driver's seat of your perception. Fear must pull optimism out of the seat to take its place and drive you to shit town. Let's talk about how to stop that from happening.

FEAR FACTORY

"To conquer fear is the beginning of wisdom" – Bertrand Russell.

Fear is the single most debilitating force in the human psyche. It can hide in the dark corners of your mind. If left untreated, it will flare up more and more often, threatening to overtake you. It is also a contagion that spreads at the speed of a virus. It is insurrectionary and can topple entire civilizations. Even worse, it is a subversive insurgent to your every cause. So, it is critical to address how to deal with it to ensure you are successful. You must be able to walk the unfamiliar path with concrete confidence. You need to be able to look people right in the eyes comfortably. You want to be able to sit with yourself alone and feel the most secure. You must be courageous enough to communicate to people what you believe to be true and what you want.

"The things that terrify you, as if they were about to happen, may never come; certainly, they have not come yet. Some things torment us more than they should, some before they should, some when they should not torment us at all." – Seneca.

These things and many more dramatically affect your results. Security, confidence, and attention are all quickly stifled by fear. So, it would be best if you spent considerable effort dealing with your fear. I have dealt with fear extensively, and I'll share a terrible and magnificent story about it at the end of this section. For many reasons, I have studied and practiced prescriptions for dealing with fear. However, from what I can tell, no single method is stunningly successful or complete at disarming it. In comparison, this approach is promising. Hopefully, I will get some beneficial feedback from this.

I know I'm speaking to a varied audience, so this is a bit tricky to communicate. Some of you might not be afraid of much. And others may be thinking that fear has possessed you. The reality is that you are both probably wrong if you think that way. Fear is likely the culprit for that weird behavior you do that you regret. Also, if you "worry" about any form of shortcoming, you have fear. If you feel jealous or angry, you have fear underneath those feelings, even though they are different emotions. We all have fear, which is normal. But you also are not being crushed by fear. Fear cannot crush you unless you stand underneath it. You make fear, and it comes exclusively from inside you. Let us backtrack first and deal with it a bit so it doesn't stop you from being able to listen well.

Here is the uncomfortable part. It's important to admit you have fear so it comes into the view of your awareness. You can do it. Remember, awareness is your weapon against subversion. In other words, nothing is hidden that is being observed. The power of fear is significantly reduced by awareness alone. This is the **first step** to facing your fears. You must look right at them, honestly. This is especially useful when you feel it coming on strong. Stop thinking and acting for a minute and fix your internal gaze on that feeling. Don't try to run from it; realize you are the source of it. Look that son of a bitch right in the proverbial eyes, and don't say or think anything at first. Mindfully observe. Use your insight meditation training to disconnect from your thoughts. This will create some space between you and your fear and allow you to observe it without feeling it. That's it, it's that simple. Stare at it objectively and non-descriptively with your internal gaze and attention. Notice it getting smaller.

The truth is that you can find a reason to be afraid every second of your life. There are a million ways anything around you or inside you can go terribly wrong at any moment. It's amazing that we have that knowledge and are not terrified to live. Instead, we are courageous to live despite our omnipotence of ever-present entropy. We do it by not thinking about how things could go wrong and choosing to think about what we can do to make things go to plan, even if we must make adjustments along the way. I believe this is the essence of optimism, which is the most powerful and underrated idea for creating success, as I previously discussed.

You must adopt a proper conceptualization of what fear is. That is to understand what it is and what it isn't. As a very young person, I thought of fear as elusive. So, I was attracted to Jiddu Krishnamurti's perspective on fear. He believed fear is a product of your imagination. You are the one who makes your fear; it isn't something outside of you that creeps in or happens to you. Fear can't sneak up behind you and jump on you. If you try to describe the qualities of fear, you only end up describing your experience. You can't describe fear itself because it doesn't exist in the material world. You can't see it with your eyes or under a microscope; it has no smell, taste, sound, weight, energy, or anything one can measure. So, Krishnamurti has suggested to stop saying, "I am afraid," and start saying, "I am making fear." You should try this. It works very well in several ways to diminish your fear's power. And it is one of the best practices for taking responsibility.

I agree that fear comes from us, and we often make it for completely inappropriate, imaginary, and even delusional reasons. But, even though it's illusive, fear is real, and its response is uniquely observable in our bodies. It is a deep biological reaction. That's what makes it tricky. It is primarily an unconscious and autonomous reaction. So, you can't kill it. It's part of you. Also, you wouldn't want to kill it completely. It is useful for detecting danger and instantly enabling you to deal with it psychologically and physiologically (mentally and physically). The impulse of fear signals us to exercise caution, like when we walk too close to the edge of a cliff. But immediately after the impulse, fear is no longer helpful. Reasoning is the best way to exercise caution. Being afraid of falling off a cliff after you are away from the edge is unreasonable. Being afraid of falling off that cliff later that night while trying to sleep is supremely useless. This example is obvious, but we do that very thing with fear of rejection, failure, confrontation, change, uncertainty, inadequacy, etc.

The fear response is a damn impressive mechanism. It's a miracle that has undoubtedly saved the extinction of each of us and our entire species countless times. It is probably the most expensive miracle of our evolution, however. The cost of our fear response saving our lives is measured by all the times it inappropriately prevented us from taking opportunities when the risk was worth it. The best example is being too afraid to trust and attacking first. This leaves the other person or people in a position limited to only counterattack or evasion. That process grows, spreads, and validates fear. This is how we turn a little insecurity into a divorce, invasion, or any kind of otherwise unnecessary war. That process is costly. So, if fear is so good and so bad, what do we do about it? I use a couple of principal ways of thinking about fear that seems accurate, useful, and simple enough to remember.

1. <u>Our fear response poorly distinguishes between actual or imagined stimuli.</u> Compared to thinking about being under attack, what happens inside your body when you are actually under attack is almost identical. You can see a grizzly bear in the distance and not have to wait until it is attacking you to experience a fear response. Otherwise, you might decide to pet the cute fluffy guy.

2. <u>The validity and utility of fear decline rapidly with any increase in the complexity of the stimulus.</u> In other words, our fear response is more like a switch or a trigger attempting to deal with an environment of ever-varying degrees and increasing complexity. So, if a bear attack video was recorded, uploaded, and then viewed, you could experience a fear response similar to being attacked yourself. However, you are just watching glowing pixels on a screen change color rapidly. This is a little less valid but still can be helpful because your fear response is helping you permanently learn that you are scared to death to be attacked by a bear. But how valid and practical is a fear response when a friend texts you something they heard, suggesting someone else may post a picture of you doing something that may reflect poorly on you? It's much less valid because the threat can't be verified. Furthermore, fear becomes entirely invalid and useless when you start imagining things going wrong for you for which there is no evidence.

Fear becomes unreliable when applied abstractly. Further, it causes a destructive condition for your success in anything. If you start imaginatively thinking of any of the millions of things that could go wrong but aren't going wrong, you are abstracting fear into a realm where it is completely useless and harmful. I concede that when imagining things to fear abstractly, a person will be right occasionally. But being right, one time out of a hundred or a thousand is far from reliable. That is proof that the strategy is unreliable. Further, it's entirely possible to unintentionally influence or manifest the conditions for a fear to come true because one is looking for it and giving it so much attention. The basic rule to remember is that if there is much at all to think about, making fear is making it worse. Insert reason, logic, and intuition instead. Or insert faith, which seems the same as optimism to me.

3. You need to recover from every fear response.

Being afraid pushes your body and your mind very hard. You get dosed with adrenaline and cortisol, a stress hormone. Your heart rate and blood pressure get elevated. Your blood flow changes away from your heart and into your limbs, preparing you to fight or run. Your muscles tense up. The area of your brain where reason and judgment come from gets impaired. Rational thought gets more difficult. You will feel alert, agitated, and argumentative. It doesn't last long, and it can take up to an hour or more to recover afterward. During recovery, you will come down from the experience and go lower than before for a while. You will have fatigue, hormone imbalance, and maybe even body pain. Your emotions and thoughts will not be optimal; thus, your decisions and actions will not be optimal. With this in mind, you don't want to be having this response constantly or inappropriately imagining reasons to respond in this way. Even after you get good at cutting out all the useless abstract fear you may be imagining, fear will still happen sometimes. You can diminish it and contain it. It is in your control. In fact, you are the only one who can control it.

What you can do about fear is bring it to the conscious level by observing it. You can face it, and it will subside to a considerable degree. And that's where we usually leave the conversation. But what the hell do you do after that? That is what I always wanted to know. Doing those two things indeed helps, but we can go further. We can apply prevention and preparation. We have determined that the simple and direct fears are valid and useful. For example, if you are being physically attacked, you will benefit by being afraid. So, we focus on reducing the abstract fear that results in a negative net result for our life experience, like being afraid that people don't like you or you aren't good enough.

Once you've mastered the regular discipline of calmly looking directly at inappropriate abstract fear when it arises and diminishing it with observation, you can employ other strategies. First, you need to have a powerful antithesis (something that is the direct opposite). The antithesis to most human abstract fear is developed in your relationship with yourself. I believe it is so because that is where genuine optimism comes from. An African proverb states, *"When there is no enemy within, the enemies outside cannot hurt you."* You need to be able to be comfortable while alone and introspective. Self-reliance, self-security, and self-worth are what you are after. These are the seeds of true strength and the death of most useless fear.

We all have a duality to us that has been described in the West since our beginnings. It was originally secularly described as a psychomachia (battle between virtue and vices for the soul of Man). It was also understood as a battle between good and evil within the heart of every person in religion, namely Christianity. Aleksandr Solzhenitsyn said, *"The line separating good and evil passes …right through every human heart…"* The point is that each of us must be honest and familiar with ourselves and then integrate the good and the bad. We must unify the beautiful and the ugly within.

There are many complicated ways to improve your relationship with yourself, and they are probably all worthwhile. However, I like to start simple. Simple doesn't mean easy; it means straightforward. The struggle is evidence that it's working and worthwhile. I like to trust and deploy our innate ability to adapt first. It's powerful, effective, and a superpower built into us. Your body and mind will always adapt to improve what they are regularly asked to do. That is useful and simple to use. So, with that in mind. You need to be able to be alone and present with yourself comfortably and confidently for thirty minutes daily. This practice isn't designed to combat the fear of loneliness but rather to develop the strongest antithesis to fear.

By alone, I mean not being on your phone, not reading, not getting lost in thought or a narrative in your imagination. No distractions are allowed. This will be more difficult than it sounds, and you may only make it a few minutes at first. That's okay; beat your time tomorrow. Improve your time each day until you can do it for thirty minutes. This may be challenging and uncomfortable. You are your own harshest critic, who knows every single undesirable thing about you. You are also the only person you need approval from. If you can get this asshole to approve of you, you will be fearless in your disposition and motion.

I will interject here that I didn't think of this next exercise. I discovered it by accident. Here is the short version that hopefully is relatable. My first wife left abruptly after thirteen years. I fell apart in every way. I got very sick due to letting my health fail, which was a far fall from a very strong, athletic, and otherwise successful young person. I moved back into my old rental house that the previous tenant destroyed. This, among many other things, was all going wrong at the same time as things tend to do. I gutted it and lived in an empty space. I had a hammock, a two-drawer nightstand with a few clothes, a journal, a few books, one towel, and one place setting, and that's about it.

I simplified life to a condition I could manage, which was not much. The shower and the drain stopper were broken, so I would take a "cup shower," where I sat in the empty bathtub, used the cup to harness the running water, and rinsed off. I couldn't even muster up the motivation to fix the tap. Fixing myself was an impossible notion. Also, none of my friends or family ever really showed up, and I didn't know how to ask them for support. I was terrible at accepting any help. I had no idea what this was about or even had a spare bit of energy to spend on it. It was just the way it needed to be. All I had was myself, space, and time. As it turns out, self, space, and time are the fertile ground of the universe. I didn't know up from down, and my emotions were too intense to be reliable or tolerable. I had no idea what to do or not do.

One day, after taking a cup-shower and looking down at my naked self, I noticed that I was looking thin. So, I decided to look in the mirror. Immediately, I was aghast. I did not know this person in the mirror at all. Something inside me seemed to split open, and while I was appalled and afraid, I couldn't pull my eyes off myself. But I couldn't look into my own eyes. I now had a goal. I needed to be able to look myself in the eyes. This was something I needed to be able to do, even if I didn't know why. Little by little, day by day, I got to know myself. I must have had dozens of naked conversations with myself in that mirror. We would cry together, laugh together, dance together, have terrible confrontations, and sometimes even throw hands at each other. After replacing a couple of broken mirrors, our conversations turned from tumultuous to cooperative in a short time. Soon after, we didn't have much left to say to each other than simple encouragement.

Finally, I had nothing to say or feel when I looked in the mirror. Yeah, I may have lost my shit there for a bit, but you can't lie to yourself and pretend you have yourself together. Period. I got to know myself and made a best friend of me. When I walked out of that house after finally having myself on my side, I was unstoppable. I moved from being in my own way to watching my back, and subsequently, the whole world fell to its knees for me immediately. It was an even more ethereal and beautiful experience than that, but I don't want to spoil the experience for you.

Each one of you will have to start at a different point. If you are a little insecure, you may need to wear a nice outfit and be fully presentable to sit with yourself for a few minutes. It's a strange notion meeting yourself. Take it seriously; you will never meet a more important person in your life for your life. Do it at first in whatever way you think will make you the most accepting of yourself.

Start with focusing your attention on your breathing and then move your attention to each of your senses one at a time. Listen to the sounds around you in the distance, the smells in the air, the feelings on your skin, etc. Do it every day. There is a little place of natural power inside of you that will start to wake up and grow. It may be like a little puddle of water at first, and you are now making rain across the watershed of your entire being. Once you can make it to thirty minutes, push further and become more vulnerable. Move in front of a full-length mirror. Wear less clothing, jewelry, and makeup. Don't fix your hair.

When you can be alone and present, comfortably and confidently, while standing in front of a mirror completely raw and naked, unafraid to stare into your own eyes, you become a deadly force in life. Talk to yourself in the mirror. Tell yourself the truth. Call out your lies and bury them. Be kind to the person in the mirror and offer to help them with whatever they need and mean it. Ask yourself for forgiveness and give it. Ask yourself for encouragement and approval and give it. Asking and giving are both difficult and uncomfortable; do them anyway. Keep going, get to know this person, and work out all the shit between you. I know it sounds crazy; stop thinking about that. Be consistent with this practice. The two of you will become one. This is the battle to defeat all enemies capable of sabotaging your success in life. This is the end of your diminishing duality.

Together with your reflection, decide what's right and wrong, good and bad, what you must stop doing, and what you must do. Put them in a hierarchy or order of importance. Of course, you can rely on outside wisdom or spiritual guidance with this part if you wish. Be honest because you will find your power in the truth and discover that it is nothing to fear. Speak not what you want to hear but what you need to hear. When you operate in truth, you move in alignment with reality, and all opposition will falter. If you find out that you don't know the truth about yourself, as you certainly will, find out where exactly and commit to seeking it.

Your little puddle of life force will become a raging river. You will find that you can look at all your parts, into your own eyes, and off into the distance without distinctions of thought or emotion. Over time, you will become familiar with this place inside of you and develop an enormous affinity for it. You will carry it with you everywhere you go. Now, you are flowing and raging on the inside with potential energy. On the outside, you will seem to have a powerful stillness. People will be attracted to and intimidated by it. They will react differently to you, especially because you won't be reacting to them much at all unless you decide to. You know exactly who you are and who you aren't. Your river can easily wash away any trash that someone throws in it. You feel completely comfortable looking into someone else's eyes and can watch how they feel your river flow. You will find that you zap the inauthentic power out of some people, and they crumble in front of you without a word from your mouth. This may be a new responsibility for you.

People you previously may have felt deserved retribution, punishment, or failure will likely be weak in front of you now. You will feel sorry for them. It will be easy to replace your ill will toward someone with sympathy for them. They must live with themselves. That's their karma. Or when you are ready, notice that you now feel inspired to encourage them somehow. But you never have to let them impose upon you or anyone you care about again. You will have no issue confronting them calmly and assertively with a deadly presence.

You will also discover incredibly awesome people with ease. Often, some will have been near you the whole time. Your network just found a direct path to becoming unbelievably powerful and ripe with genuine reciprocity. You will now have something to offer that the best of people will desire. You will now be able to properly receive anything positive offered to you. This is how I was ready and available to fall in love with my wife, Lindsey, and our new relationship was incendiary as a result.

Once you get to the thirty-minute mark, you can relax your daily practice if you want. Be sure to maintain your relationship with yourself. Like a good friend, check on yourself once or twice weekly. You will look forward to it. Your small behaviors are what you want to focus on now and forever. You can't jump back into life the same way you did before, or you will regress. Now, you can look fear right in the eyes, so be sure to always look people right in the eyes—present good posture. Speak with conviction. Be decisive and admit when you are wrong. Listen without excess emotional reaction, and don't let yourself be baited into dramatics. Hold your aim steady like a sniper or a surgeon. You will now be best positioned to seek out and dive into struggles and challenges enthusiastically. They will be a warm blanket for you.

All right, here is my terrible and beautiful story of being forced to face fear. I was around seven years old, a little while after my parents split up. My younger siblings and I lived in a government-subsidized apartment complex with my mom. That is basically the Midwest version of the projects. I used to walk down the dark, musty, carpeted stairs to the basement laundry room to have some space to play. I was a small boy, and it was too dangerous to go outside or to the playground alone. Places like this are where all the nefarious characters end up living together. It's kind of like a kindergarten for prison life and street life. So, the rule at the time was that I had to stay in the building. I didn't mind; I liked the laundry room. I didn't understand anything about this kind of danger. I had lived in a rural country house with a big yard for the first six years of my life. We had a couple of friendly neighbors who also let me play at their homes. The only danger I had experienced until then was getting scratches while playing outside. It was an excellent place to be a young kid.

The complex was different, and I soon realized just how different it was. The laundry room had doors on two sides, leading to a half flight of stairs up to exit doors. It seemed to keep me close to home but away from danger. However, those doors couldn't stop monsters from coming in. While playing with some tiny toy cars called micro-machines, I heard one of those heavy, squeaky doors open. In walked an oversized boy and his extra fat sister. They were probably somewhere around twelve years old.

Immediately, I could tell they were different somehow, and I didn't want them to notice me. Unfortunately, they did.

The brother started aggressively saying things to me I didn't understand. I didn't even know enough about life to be afraid. I just stayed quiet. Then, he started pushing me to the ground. I tried to flee, but he would grab me and throw me to the ground. The more I tried to get away, the harder he would beat me. I looked to his sister for help, but she was laughing and grinning. Just then, I heard someone open an exit door. I saw a figure through the laundry door window, and I screamed for help. I remember the person's head poking up, looking, and then him walking up the stairs indifferently. Immediately after calling for help, the sister was on top of me, covering my mouth with one hand and strangling me with the other. I woke from the blackout to being repeatedly smacked by her.

For over an hour, I was a captive of two completely insane and violent pre-teens who must have experienced more pain than I can imagine. They were unloading it all on me. I was an easy target at seven years old, fifty pounds wet. Minutes felt like hours. They beat me repeatedly. Anything I did would trigger them. If I didn't do anything, it triggered them. If I made eye contact, I got it the worst. There was no way out; no one was going to help me. I went through every kind of emotion, most of which I had never felt before. To say that I was terrified would be a dramatic understatement. They were yelling crazy things at me the whole time, but the only thing I understood was that they were never going to let me go. That was the most important thing they wanted me to understand. That was also their mistake. They left me no way to surrender. I would have, no doubt about it. But it wasn't an available choice.

After dozens of beatings, I gave up and stopped trying to defend myself. They kept beating me, but I became calm. I could still feel the pain, but it didn't bother me anymore. My gaze was fixed on my blood spattered on the floor with some weird wipe shapes and a shoe print. I looked at it but no longer had thoughts and felt no feelings. Something inside me died; my light went out, but the darkness left behind wasn't empty. An immense and terrible beast was waking up and waiting in the shadows inside me. I could feel that monstrous animal step into my being and become me.

I pushed myself to my feet and ran straight at the boy first. He anticipated me running for the door again and was surprised and off balance as I quickly got to him. Even though he was three times my size, I ran through him like a grizzly bear and landed on top of him. I tore at him like a wild animal. The sounds that came out of me will ring in my memory always. I wasn't fighting him; I was destroying him. I scratched at the softness of his eyes, bit him wherever he grabbed me, and threw my quick, tiny fists and claws anywhere they would land.

His sister grabbed me from behind and pulled me off, but she had hesitated long enough for me to damage him considerably. I bit her finger and felt it crush between my teeth, and I refused to let it go even when she released me. I was gnashing my teeth and shaking my head, trying to tear her finger off. She fell to the ground in agony and surrendered, but my beast knew no mercy. I stomped her face until she became quiet and motionless. I wanted to crush that devious smile and smash it into the concrete forever. As I looked over her unconscious face, quietly gasping for breaths, I heard her brother whimpering. He was crawling for the door because his eyes no longer worked. I let out a little laugh at this. There was no way I was letting him get away. I kicked him until my body couldn't pick up my foot anymore. I felt nothing other than regret that I couldn't hurt them more. I enjoyed breaking them and took pleasure in listening to his pleas and desperate begging.

I remember recovering from this experience and thinking about it as a child. I remember my fear of those children, but I was most scared of myself. I was afraid people would find out what I had done. I was afraid of what I would do next. Fortunately, my beast retreated into my shadows, but he was no longer sleeping. We have a strange relationship, my beast and me. I don't trust him, but he also brings me peace. When I call on him, he always answers. He never pokes his head up and walks away indifferently. And he is content to rest in my shadows until I need him.

We all have a beast inside. It is made of fire and darkness. It is sleeping in some of us. That's okay; hopefully, you never need to wake it up. Just know that it is there, and it is terribly more powerful than fear itself. Fear is prey for shadow beasts. You are built to face fear and overcome it. If you need to, look at your fear through the eyes of your beast, and your fear will run for its life. Your beast knows no retreat from a meal. When you feel the hand of fear squeezing your chest and begin to lose hope, you can ask your beast to bite off its fingers, and with only a whisper, your beast will feast.

HAPPINESS AND CONFIDENCE

Everyone wants to be happy and live in happiness. It's more than a want; it is an important principle idea that was even grounded in the US Declaration of Independence as an unalienable right. The idea seems simple enough, but I still haven't met anyone who doesn't find happiness elusive at times. Even in the US Declaration, the pursuit of happiness was designated as what we wanted instead of only happiness itself. It appears the word happiness back then also reflected our constant disagreement and confusion about its meaning and was correlated to matters of estate. That certainly illustrates our belief that happiness comes with the gain of things we value outside ourselves. We persistently believe this even though the evidence to support it remains absent. I'm using Western examples here, but this unicorn-chasing behavior by humans is found in most cultures in different ways.

"Most people mistakenly equate pleasure with happiness, leading to a shallow existence. Superior individuals find happiness in honor rather than mere pleasure." – Aristotle.

We need to delete the correlation we imagine between pleasure and happiness. They both feel good, but it seems to me pleasure has become a tool of expedience. Expedience means being convenient and practical despite possibly being improper or immoral. We want to feel pleasure, and we want to experience happiness. Both are important, and we are good at becoming efficient at doing things that are good and important. But when we try to become efficient at achieving happiness, we often end up being expedient at obtaining pleasure instead. That is a dangerous confusion, even though it is only a slight distinction. It's like holding a knife upside down by accident. It's a small error, but a huge problem when you put your hand on top to apply pressure.

There is an enormous difference between doing cocaine off a

stranger's naked body and receiving the Nobel Peace Prize. However, both would feel good in a remarkably similar way in the same part of our brain. So, I find it best to figure out pleasure versus happiness and keep them in separate boxes. The pleasure box should only be opened with caution, and don't dig too deep because you won't find a Nobel Peace Prize in there. The best way to tell the difference is to become truly present. Meditate for a second, clear your mind, and observe. Happiness will rush into a person who is present and mindful every time. However, the empty desire for simple pleasure will subside with mindfulness. Also, true happy feelings grow bigger with the process of tending to their conditions. So, it's best not to try to be efficient at receiving happiness. Just look forward to it while it is absent. As *this too shall pass*, happiness shall return soon enough.

"There is nothing in the world so much admired as a man who knows how to bear unhappiness with courage." – Seneca.

One of my favorite explanations of this distinction comes from clinical psychologist, author, professor, and public speaker Dr. Jordan Peterson. He stated that positive emotions from satiation are immediately destroyed, but positive emotions from incentives can be lasting. To be satiated is to be satisfied fully. To be incentivized is to be encouraged and motivated. Unearned pleasure is usually a positive emotion, but it destroys itself as soon as you satiate that desire. So, you end up putting effort into creating the desire or need constantly instead of putting energy into executing and sustaining the positive feeling. You then spend almost all your time wanting instead of having. This is not happiness. In contrast, happiness is usually related to positive emotions based on actions or thoughts that can keep expanding with frequency. These positive emotive experiences themselves are the incentive. So, you get to focus your energy on experiencing the positive emotion and its growth.

To say it another way - stop setting off bombs of pleasure and start tending the fire of happiness. Have a sustained positive experience instead of tension in anticipation. Both bombs and fires start with a spark, but a fire will sustain and grow with the right kind of attention. Also, a fire can become much more sensational than a bomb ever could if given enough encouragement.

Biology can explain why the human race has been focused on happiness with no progress to speak of. The relationship forces of selection in humans cause some confusion between success and happiness. We want relationships. We choose partners for all relationships by biological indicators of health and success of some kind. We want to be chosen more than anything. So, we want to gain indicators of health and success to present to people as much as we want to have them for ourselves. When we can possess anything that a culture agrees is valuable, then we are satisfying a condition for that deep desire to be accepted and chosen.

I'm not an evolutionary biologist, and I'm aware that science gets foggy with humans. But, if we hold the connection I just illustrated as a loose representation of a truth, it is safely functional. There are other ways to look at why we want success. However, when you look at why we want success in this way, you can see it isn't a bad thing, but it also isn't happiness. Being successful by gaining "valuable" things can help create a condition beneficial for happiness in the satisfaction of a primary need. But it certainly doesn't guarantee any level of happiness. To start with, only one condition is satisfied, and material success also brings burden.

Anyone without material success often doesn't account for or appreciate the burdens that can come with it. Maybe there are worse problems a person could have, but maybe they are much more difficult than one would expect. For example, the ability to take any reward at any time can make it difficult to be driven or motivated toward the next worthwhile endeavor. We have already discussed the absolutely essential nature of seeking treasure. Having excess access to comfort and pleasure sounds like a victory, but it's actually the beginning of an epic battle for your soul. When you can afford to replace all the meaningful things in life with meaningless purchases, you might do that because it is easier. If you fall in love with your influence or power, you may become only that. You will be constantly in danger from yourself and need awareness more than ever.

Also, there are a surprising amount of parasitic people out there just waiting around every corner to take your success from you or benefit from it in some way. That leads to making new connections, which is a stressful and risky endeavor. It can become very difficult to trust people or make new friends, always wondering if they are into you or just hoping to gain from you. If you aren't careful, success can bring you the strangest type of crowded loneliness. Furthermore, you become a target of people's envy, and many will help you slip up and fail to make themselves feel better. So, you are always under investigation or at risk of attack, and it can be suffocating. The trick to having material wealth and still being happy is to learn how to be happy first.

Happiness isn't found in unnecessary things of monetary value. Think of happiness like a flower. If you buy a flower arrangement, you will enjoy it briefly and then watch it die. However, if you create the right conditions for a flowering plant to grow and bloom instead, you get to enjoy that flower bloom longer and with much deeper regard for a fraction of the price of an arrangement. If you create those conditions in many places throughout your space with many types of plants, then you have flowers to enjoy most of the time. That is an ethereal experience.

Like gardening, creating the conditions for deep, genuine happiness takes a little work and getting your hands dirty. It also requires consistent love and attention. Most of all, it requires patience. If you know what these conditions are and learn to enjoy working on them, you will successfully create many blooms of happiness. In either case, if you do well, genuine people will want to come to your garden.

If it sounds unpleasant to you to do hard, dirty work to be happy, then you need to keep working on changing your mind and learning to love struggle. Calmly doing work, cultivating, and getting dirty in itself can bring you all the pleasure and happiness you could want. The blooms are a bonus. I intentionally put this chapter about happiness toward the end of *We Aren't Who We Are,* so you would best be positioned to understand what I mean.

Here is the good news. If you have read, *We Aren't Who We Are* from the beginning to this point, you already know the conditions for happiness and how to create them. They are, in fact, the same conditions for success and positive experience. Both are mutually inclusive of the experience you are looking for.

Confidence is a big part of having a positive life experience. Confidence is much like happiness in the way that you can't just make the feeling happen and expect to keep it. You must create the sustaining conditions for it within yourself. There must be some real substance to build confidence upon. At this point in our journey, you've been given the tools to build genuine and unbreakable confidence. Imagine if you were a person who could find your ignorance and could change your mind whenever you want. Imagine you also loved getting into struggles and achieving personal growth and accomplishments. Imagine further that you could influence your existence in reality with authority any time you want to align with a worthwhile goal. Also, consider if you were cognizant of your biological drives and could use them to incentivize and empower you further. Just think if you were all that and were fearless with unbending honesty, strength, and PDR. If this were a description of you and you were living that experience, you wouldn't feel anything other than confidence.

You simply cannot be averse to complete self-sovereign culpability and have a positive experience after childhood. This means you can't find happiness by putting responsibility for yourself onto your spouse, friends, boss, fans, political ideology, religious dogmas, etc. However, you can be happy and confident in a positive life experience simply by taking complete responsibility for everything about you and your life. *We Are Not Who We Are* offers the specifics on how to do that. When you accept that responsibility and the appropriate actions, success comes easily.

It is best to think of building your success by prioritizing from the foundation up. Your relationship with yourself and your health is the most essential endeavor for all types of success and happiness. Genuine quality relationships with other people are the next most valuable thing one will ever find in life. Success in forming a friendly environment and circumstances for your life endeavor is the next most useful thing. Success at working toward a worthwhile goal is then positioned favorably for victory. Getting paid well is more of a measure of success than success itself. You must have the success first to be able to measure it.

It is possible to get paid a load of money without having much of the other types of success. However, it isn't easy and won't do you any good. I've been there. You just can't buy the things you really want or will make you genuinely happy, fulfilled, complete, inspired, worthy, etc. You can't buy them, so stop trying. But you can make them, and it doesn't have to cost a thing other than effort.

Furthermore, the first thing you would do if you made a load of money is to start trying to get the other kinds of success. But it will be more difficult to do it backward, especially if the way you are getting paid is working against you. If your money-making endeavor is negatively affecting your health, personal progress, or relationships, it is working against you becoming successful. For example, if you work 80+ hours a week, the foundation of your overall life will likely be frail and easily collapse with the first strong wind. If you are pimping, prostituting, selling addictive drugs, writing fake news or clickbait, etc., you can get paid a lot of money, but you will have a nearly impossible chance of being successful in life. If you are willing to lower the value of your character to increase pay, you are doing the opposite of becoming valuable to yourself. And you matter; your character is important to me, to you, and to everyone.

It is so much easier and better to get paid doing something you believe is worthwhile and honorable. It's even better if it aligns with what you truly want and love. And man, when you do it the right way, it is an incredible experience! Thankfully, I've been there as well. You can still buy some things for fun, no problem. Fun is good. Buying fun is good if you can afford it. Most people I meet don't even know what they can afford. You should know how to keep a financial plan with budgets.

Yeah, you have to pay the bills, so making changes may sound difficult. Make your bills as small as possible, stop buying frivolous things you don't really want, and free up energy and time to start making moves for real successes you approve of. Two ways to increase your income-to-debt ratio are to make more money and spend less money. If you do both, you can create some wiggle room very quickly. Most people in the West seem to forget that spending less increases their available income immediately. If that extra available income is then applied to reducing debt further and any increase in pay you earn along the way is applied to reducing debt as well, you will have started a compounding cycle that will free you from debt quickly. If you have large financial obligations that you can live without and you discover that they don't actually give your life special meaning or functionality, sell them. Sell them at a loss if you must. Pay off that loss over time and consider it a victory over indentured servitude.

Here is a fun challenge: Look over last month's banking statements and categorize all the money you spent. Now rewrite these categories as budgets (the maximum amount you can spend every month), but enter the value as half as much as last month. Budget yourself to spend half as much on every category possible. Measure your worth at how successful you can be at hitting your budgets. You will, of course, start with the easiest and quickest categories. Then you will have leftover money on your balance. It becomes possible if you stick to your goal and use that extra money to pay down another obligation to lower your payment. After you pay it down, you have even more available money, and the following debt obligation becomes even faster and easier to pay off. And that momentum grows. It may seem to start slowly but will accelerate if you stick to it. The difficulty isn't the strategy; it's very simple. The challenge is overcoming the seduction to spend the extra money you create on frivolous things or more debt.

This book has given you the skills and strength to overcome that seduction. But I'll offer you a trick that helps make it easier. Set a transaction wait time requirement for yourself. When you want to buy something you don't need to survive, wait at least twenty-four hours to buy it. Seventy-two hours is better if you can manage. For example, if you want a fancy dinner or a new pair of shoes, pick out what you want and agree to let yourself buy it on a particular day in the future. You will satisfy that desire without spending a dollar. Then, when the day comes, review your budget and decide if you still want to buy it. Many times, that desire to buy it will have vanished entirely. This is kind of a way to disempower fleeting emotional spending.

Money may not create happiness, but crushing debt sure does create unhappiness and a unique type of bondage. Like all things, the only way to do anything about it is to take responsibility for it and do something about it. And when, or if, you are already a person free of debilitating debt, then you will have available money. Learn the difference between an asset and a liability and use your available money and credit to buy only assets. Read *Rich Dad Poor Dad* by Robert T. Kiyosaki for a basic understanding of this concept. Buy frivolous things only from the additional income of assets. This is the next step that puts you into a position of not working for the fun things you buy. Now, you are not trading your time and effort for frivolous things, but you can still have them if you want.

The primary reason to be successful at managing your money and growing your financial freedom is that it enables you to focus on things that matter to you more because you matter. The world desperately needs your unique talents and contributions. You need to use your talents and contribute to thrive. You can't even imagine how important you are to the whole of everything. You must get those chains off and start running the right way. We are all counting on you. And that is precisely where happiness is located—in the pursuit.

Happiness is in the pursuit because it is the thing in the present moment, and that is where we need to give our attention. As I said before, focus all the power and quality of your attention on what is in front of you right now as often as possible. Right now is the only thing you have. I like how neuroscientist, philosopher, and author Samuel Harris explained this truth in a very objective way in a lecture. He said,

"The past is a memory. It is a thought arising in the present. The future is merely anticipated; it is another thought arising now. What we truly have is this moment, and this, and this, …. And we spend most of our lives forgetting this truth, repudiating it, fleeing it, overlooking it. And the horror is that we succeed. We manage to never connect with the present moment and find fulfillment there. Because we are continually hoping to become happy in the future. And the future never arrives. Even when we think we are in the present moment, we are, in very subtle ways, looking over its shoulder, anticipating what's coming next. We are always solving a problem. And it's possible to simply drop your problem, if only for a moment, and enjoy whatever is true of your life in the present. This is not a matter of new information or more information. It requires change in attitude. It requires a change in the attentiveness you pay to your experience in the present moment."

DO THINGS DIFFERENTLY

We often make our drive for social acceptance into a problem for ourselves. It can inhibit us from taking ourselves through the complete execution of our plans, which is the last step in making a lasting personal change toward true success. We often decide to make a meaningful change, plan how to do it, and then chicken out when it comes time to do it because of what others will think.

We have a desire to be accepted by the group. Whatever group we are around—family, work group, social media followers, friend group, hobby group, etc. The problem is that most groups' majority consensus on what is normal, acceptable, and cool can easily be incompatible with your chosen path of personal progress. You can identify this quickly for yourself. Suppose the group norms are negativity, conflict seeking, complaining, gossip, comparing victim stories, providing each other with sympathy for trespasses to entitlement, comparing failures as if they were valuable collectibles, etc. In that case, you can't get a positive experience by fitting in with this group. You absolutely cannot let this misery become your goal and aim. It would be best if you didn't feed your desire to be accepted by this group on their terms. However, as I said before, you also cannot repress your drives, such as the desire to be accepted. So, here are the choices.

1. Only participate in groups with a positive culture. That is, if they lift each other up, support new and old ideas logically, intelligently question the status quo, expect people to progress, have discussions instead of fights, spend more time talking about events and ideas rather than people, etc. It may be impossible for you to leave some of your groups and find these. Ditch the rotten ones wherever you can and do it immediately. Your life depends on it.

2. If you have no choice but to be around people failing themselves, work to influence them instead of letting them affect you. You can do this in a way that will create a higher level of acceptance and position in the group without negatively affecting

you.

Please don't talk about any of this with them. Simply start doing things differently with confidence. Ironically, we are afraid of appearing foolish or crazy by being different in a group that repeats poor behaviors, expecting a different result somehow. It is best not to join them in their thinking if you must keep their company. You have to show them what you're doing. Be quick to disagree politely and have solid limits. For example, when someone starts talking shit, shut them down. Tell people straight up *"I don't want to gossip about anyone. I don't want to complain about this incredible life with unlimited possibilities. I don't think our boss is an asshole"* (if that's the truth).

Choose to talk about the qualities of your interests, spouse, kids, and life you like. Refuse to be subjected to anything that doesn't fit your vision. Now, that doesn't mean avoiding things you disagree with. If you inspect closely, it will be evident that you need new ideas. Just avoid negative tribalistic bullshitters selling ideological membership. Push back, be consistent and confident. Most people will admire you for it after they work through their emotional responses, and most will hold you in higher regard than ever before. Regardless, you will hold yourself in higher esteem, which matters most.

From here on out, it is going to get weird. And that is exactly what you want.

Big patterns are made of small patterns, and small patterns are made of even smaller connections. The patterns of our behavior are related to the patterns of our thoughts, and they are both affected by and affect the neural pathways in our brains. That much we know for sure. We can change our minds, and our minds can change how we think and behave. Our thoughts and actions are everything regarding our experience and results in life. So, when you consider what you are thinking about and what actions you are taking, you are considering absolutely everything accessible to you. There is no mundane thought or action. They are all intensely affecting and changing you. They are you.

What makes humans special is that we can be aware of our impulses, thoughts, and behaviors. We can watch them happen as they happen from an objective perspective. That's really weird and tremendously powerful if you think about it. That awareness then provides us a choice of how to respond to stimuli that arise, like thoughts that pop in your head, words that hit your ears, sights you see, biological motivations, etc. That choice is available thousands of times per day as internal and external stimuli appear. If we hold a forward intention and awareness, we can respond in a consistently chosen direction. This direction will then influence your movement and orientation, yielding additional stimuli favorable and relevant to your intention. This is how we take responsibility and control of our destiny and cause it to compound. If your intention is honest, honorable, righteous, virtuous, or whatever upward aiming adjective you prefer, your will becomes the inflection point that recurves your existence toward success. Who are you? You can define yourself by looking at your decisions of how you respond to impulses and stimuli. Who will you become?

The most unsuccessful person chooses to avoid awareness in the first place. The most successful person works to stay objectively aware, has a vision in mind, and holds a forward intention that directs their response to impulse and stimuli.

We Aren't Who We Are has been mostly about responding differently to yourself and your environment, thus making new connections, patterns, thoughts, and behaviors toward a different, improved experience and results. However, much of my approach has been to let the old you die or fade away like an extinction process. The methods you have read here can make enormous positive changes for you in thirty to ninety days, depending on your effort. The changes will be very sticky, and you will keep most of them with reasonable effort. If you continue the practices for six months to a year, you will have made a permanent change. And that is my recommendation for how to make changes in yourself for yourself.

However, this process can be accelerated from an extinction

process to an extinction event. There are ways to unwire yourself very rapidly. Before mentioning these next methods to anyone, I recommend that they read this book first. Unwiring oneself without a rewiring plan can make things worse.

There are a few ways to unwire yourself exceptionally rapidly. These aren't magic pills; they are difficult, uncomfortable, and possibly painful. Killing the old you quickly will hurt. There is no reason to consider an extreme method if you don't need an extreme change immediately and aren't willing to accept the risks that come with it. Extreme methods aren't practical. However, in the spirit of being forthcoming and the general love of knowledge, I'll share some things I have learned from my uncanny and often irresponsible willingness to take risks.

One way to short-wire yourself is to change everything you possibly can as fast as possible and do everything differently. That is, change every action you take as much as possible. For example, read *We Aren't Who We Are*, then pick a day to move to a new place, sleep upside down in the bed, wake up at a different time, get dressed differently in all new clothes, go for a jog instead of having coffee, change your mode of transportation, walk backward all day, only interact with new people, write notes instead of talking for a while, don't talk for a day, eat only new food to you, listen to all new music, swim with your clothes on (don't drown), etc. You don't need anyone's permission to go and be as weird as you want. You have about 60,000 waking seconds in a day. If you can make most of them a novel experience for a short time, regardless of the quality, you can short out your system. We already know this to some degree and correctly call it a new start, and it has an interesting but temporary reset button effect.

For practical consideration, implementing some degree of this method can get you the "new start" effect without moving, divorcing, or being ridiculed. Do as many things as possible differently for a short while. Let go of convention or doing it right, best, or most efficient for a bit. Remember, you aren't looking to make sense here; this is to trip the expectation circuit breaker and disrupt your patterns. When you are outside your conventions and patterns, you can see them more clearly and learn where to insert new ones. It's worth asking yourself as often as possible, "Why do I do this this way."

I'll share my experience many years ago when I felt trapped and apathetic. I decided I needed to change things but didn't know what. So, I started walking to work even though that is extremely rare where I live due to unpredictable weather. It changed my perspective throughout the whole day. I didn't feel like a mindless robot lost in fantasy or apathy for a change. I felt like I could influence the outcome of my day and then behaved that way. I was like I had brought myself to work with me for the first time in a year. However, soon, I got used to the daily walk, and it lost the effect. So, I walked different paths, which renewed my openness and fresh perspective. When all the routes became familiar, I decided to walk backward, facing where I was leaving instead of where I was going, and that was a fantastic bit of experiential evidence that novelty can illicit openness.

Try it for yourself, but don't fall or walk into traffic. I'm sure it would have taken a while to get used to that way of walking, and I was at risk of getting injured, so I abandoned it and started the cycle over and drove to work. To my surprise, after a period of absence, driving to work seemed like a new, novel experience lacking in familiarity. To this day, I still change up how I get to where I'm going sometimes to recalibrate expectations and remember that I make the rules for me.

It works because of the novel stimulus. Novel means new and unusual in an interesting way. By doing only this in an immersive way, your brain, thoughts, and behaviors switch into a different mode. This mode is like relinquishing expectations and searching for new ones with a heightened sense of openness and awareness. It's like breaking out of the prison of convention. Those are precisely the conditions you want to download your new vision into. Please do it for a day or two and spend time in your vision to accelerate change. This isn't a good medium- or long-term practice, but it is a surprisingly useful short-term exercise to kick yourself out of ruts.

Perhaps you don't want to uproot your whole persona and act like a weirdo in front of everyone. That's completely sensible if it has much of good quality to your new vision. But if you still want to accelerate the unwiring process, take a trip and extend it if possible. Make the destination as foreign as possible and as long as you can afford. Going alone is essential, but that raises the risk to your safety. That is just an important part of it. Vulnerability and self-reliance are necessary. You are responsible for yourself.

To make the trip cheaper and better, backpack. That doesn't necessarily mean a hike, although a pilgrimage never hurts anyone's spirit. Just pack what you need to survive so you can still carry it easily and get off a plane or drive somewhere exotic and unfamiliar. It doesn't have to be luxurious; it's better that it isn't. I like exotic locations with a terrible economy. It's a cheap and honest experience. Backpacking is always moving forward and never staying in one place too long. So, you get the novel stimulus constantly. Your expectations are shattered, and you remain in that mode of openness.

Go ahead and research the area in advance, but plan as little as possible. Make a list of potential places to stay in certain areas, know the numbers for help, essential sentences in the language you may need, etc. But don't make a tourist itinerary. Go with the flow and make your way in whatever direction feels right. Things won't always turn out comfortably, but sometimes they will blow your mind with how amazing it is. Both are good. Back yourself into a corner in the dark, so to speak. Force yourself to adapt quickly and constantly.

Most people are often too afraid to take this type of trip for safety reasons or say it is too expensive. But ask yourself, "Am I one of the same people who risk their lives daily in "normal" ways and spend loads of money on other "important" things, none of which are serving me?" It's likely the unknown you are afraid of, but that unknown is precisely what you need to trip your wires if that's what you want to do. It is safer to do things that are within your known expectations. But you can't escape those expectations without taking a risk. Your debilitating patterns are embedded in what is comfortable to you. They are inseparable. It's your call. If you have practiced the exercises and ideas in this book for a little while, you will probably have the strength to feel confident about taking this kind of trip. Let me give you an example from my first backpacking trip.

My wife was selected as a contestant on CBS's Survivor 28 Philippines. I had to sign this comprehensive nondisclosure agreement not to communicate a single detail about it, or I would have to pay CBS $5 million that I didn't have. We were very social, so to avoid lying daily, we told everyone we were going on an extended vacation together. Our daughter went to her grandparents, my wife went to the Philippines, and I landed in San Jose, Costa Rica, with only a backpack. As I walked from the airport, a taxi driver asked where I was going. I asked him which way was good, and that was the extent of my planning. He reluctantly pointed in a direction, and I set off.

I was in my thirties and wasn't overly intentional about making improvements with this trip. But, from the beginning, I was attracted to the idea of not needing anything. Maybe this will be relatable to you. Just before the trip, I had gotten more comfortable in my life than ever before, and I noticed that I had started needing something all the time. I noticed that I had constantly created these patterns of "needing" something. I couldn't just be still as I had been most of my life previously. The extreme hustle and sense of urgency I had to create in my professional life wired me in a way that entered my whole perception. This is the entrepreneur's curse. Even at home, I had to think about something, drink coffee, smoke a cigarette, find a conversation, or do any task. I missed my stillness and didn't like this feeling of insatiability. So, my itinerary for this trip was to be still while moving about.

It worked magic on me more than I ever could have imagined. So, I reflected much about why it was so impactful. I was immediately able to fall into stillness in a new environment and didn't feel like I needed much of anything other than the essentials of life. I kicked caffeine and nicotine addiction like they were never there during the trip's first few days, which I would have never thought possible. I started meditating in strange places or just being still and watching the world move around me without feeling the need to engage. No one knew who I was or who I was supposed to be. I did not need to present myself or perform socially in any way. It seemed like a vast opening of space appeared for me just to be me. I noticed the richness of my sensory experience growing, and my desire for urgency and control melted away. I could see better and more things with more vibrant colors. I could smell all the interesting new things around me and noticed every sound. I could feel the gentle breeze whip across my skin.

Each day seemed to get longer and longer, and I was grateful for that. I didn't feel compelled to make anything happen but looked forward to simply being awake and alive. I then entered the flow of things and had the most amazing, good times with unbelievable coincidences and synchronicity. Food would seem to appear and be offered to me when I was hungry. I happened to walk out of a tree line onto a beach the very moment the setting sun touched the water. I reunited with travelers I had made friends with despite the extreme improbability of crossing paths again. Most interestingly, I never worried about much and felt good the whole time, even when caught in what I would have previously considered an uncomfortable circumstance, like sleeping outside when I mistakenly arrived in a small town after everything was closed.

I lived out of my backpack for five weeks and spent $380 while there, not including airfare. It felt like I was away for five months, and I could barely remember how I was or felt before I left. Five weeks felt like a lifetime, and I was different. I completely changed my disposition. My thoughts and behaviors after returning reflected that change, and my life experience improved. I was back in the driver's seat of me with a new sense of openness and possibility.

Another way to unwire and possibly rewire yourself simultaneously, faster than anything, is to take a psychotropic trip. That is to ingest a neurotropic or psychedelic alkaloid like the ones found in magic mushrooms, including (psilocybin) and ergot

(LSD). Or from plants such as ayahuasca (DMT), San Pedro or peyote cactus (mescaline). This isn't a recommendation to ingest any of these. This is an explanation of the observation of possible effects specific to this conversation that a human may have by ingesting one of these. These plants have existed and been used by cultures for thousands of years, so it's worth everyone knowing something about them. There is an extensive conversation to be had overall for these fascinating plants, including risks, and I have my thoughts. But I'm not going to have the whole discussion here. I will only consider what I have observed that is specific to the topic at hand. Further, scientific research now somewhat quantifies and explains many of my observations. This fascinating renewed field shows promise in teaching us more about how our mysterious consciousness works.

The effects of psilocybin temporarily shut down the areas of the brain linked to our default mode network or DMN. This is theoretically where our everyday overt conscious thought comes from, including our sense of self. This is a commonly accepted observation by modern neuroscience. See: 2016 Imperial College London neuroimaging study called "Neural correlates of the LSD experience revealed by multimodal neuroimaging," or the mounting research by Johns Hopkins University including the psychedelic effect on claustrum. I can't verify their scientific claims, but they seem clear and consistent. What we know for sure is that nearly every single person of the millions who has taken a significant dose has reported experiencing a partial or complete loss of sense of self for a few hours. This is often described as ego death. This effect is only one part of the overall state of the trip, but it is an important one. It's one of the only ways we know of to become truly objective for a sustained and consistent period of time. It's impossible even to imagine what it's like under normal circumstances. It's impossible to think about not thinking while still experiencing. But you can experience it with and without psychedelics.

Also worth noting is the DMN part of the brain is commonly found to be overactive in those suffering from depression, anxiety, and some kinds of neuroticism. So, shutting it down for a bit doesn't seem likely to hurt and is possibly a primary reason or essential contributing factor for the high success rate of this experience to be therapeutic. For our consideration, it is also advantageous. Psilocybin temporarily erases a person's old paths and patterns with one cup of tea. Of course, those paths and patterns can be found again after it wears off, but they don't have to be. This would properly position a person to pick new ones. Also, psilocybin makes one less likely to choose the same old paths and patterns because it shuts down the old ones and allows you to see the profundity and immense possibility present.

In the beginning, I told you that finding your ignorance is the key to unlocking magical doors. Psilocybin kicks the door open for you, and you can see what's on the other side. You most likely won't be able to make sense of it or know what to do about it. It isn't intelligible, justifiable, or practicable information. That's what integration support is for. That's what this book is for. You will get a glimpse and a deep experience of how small and incomplete your thinking and perception normally are compared to the vastness of life, consciousness, and possibility. What's possible will become an experience you have had instead of a concept you have thought about. A door opening for you in your perception is another way of saying you become more open. This is space for the new vision that you have created for yourself and room to do these practices.

At the same time, the DMN part of your brain and experience is shutting down; another event is coming online. This part is still unclear, but it appears that some brain regions are more stimulated, and the connective pathways are more open. There is also evidence that something about the experience enables new neurons and new neural pathways to be made surprisingly quickly compared to ordinary baseline consciousness. I don't know what will come of that research, but we do know that the experience is most often reported as profound and deeply important. Something happens that allows you to perceive the grand goings-on and experience the ineffable normally filtered out of consciousness. In other words, you have an experience so much bigger than words can describe that you can only feel it. But you don't feel it like a warm breeze; you feel it like being laboriously and sometimes painfully birthed into the rest of reality.

We know very little of what is happening scientifically during these experiences so far, and much will likely be discovered. Famous mycologist Paul Stamiz has been making claims and assisting research to prove them now for years and is getting some surprising results. Recently, a Yale study confirmed and measured the neural effects of psilocybin. "It may be the novel psychological effects of psilocybin itself that spurs the growth of neuronal connections." "We not only saw a 10 percent increase in the number of neuronal connections, but also they were on average about 10 percent larger, so the connections were stronger as well," said Yale's Alex Kwan, associate professor of psychiatry and of neuroscience and senior author of the paper. (Shao LX, Liao C, Gregg I, Davoudian PA, Savalia NK, Delagarza K, Kwan AC. Psilocybin induces rapid and persistent growth of dendritic spines in frontal cortex in vivo. Neuron. 2021 Aug 18;109(16):2535-2544.e4. doi: 10.1016/j.neuron.2021.06.008. Epub 2021 Jul 5. PMID: 34228959; PMCID: PMC8376772.)

If one were to read and practice the messages of *We Aren't Who We Are* immediately prior to an experience of this kind, it would be good preparation for psilocybin therapy. Also, if read again right after the experience for comparison, one would grasp the essence and workings of the self upon the experience from two confluent vantage points. These two vantage points in confluence create a disposition such as having both universalist and particularist views simultaneously. That's like noticing the systematic functions that apply to all life while noticing what is unique to your life and how they move together. That's where harmony is found.

It is of the greatest utility to consider both the macro and micro view of anything to understand its complexity. When trying to understand the whole of everything, it is essential to consider both the micro and macro poles (the smallest extremes and the largest as a dual starting point. This duality in cooperation is the best way to conceive of the stuff in the middle, which is everything one would want to know, especially if they were responsible for it. Just like the way we are responsible for ourselves and our lives.

However, quickly unwiring yourself isn't necessary, and no matter what you do, most of your time and effort will be focused on your rewiring. The magic is in the millions of mundane moments of everyday life where profound changes and improvements are made. The mission of this book is to stimulate experiential learning and discovery of great utility through planned and sustained voluntary exploration toward the most worthwhile goal of realizing your best vision of yourself in the world. It is you who must do this for yourself. It is done with every little step in the best direction. Every moment is an opportunity to stay true to course.

To get different results and have a different experience in life, you must change who you are to some degree. You are required to become different than you are to make a difference in who you are. That change is what manifests external results. You must be willing to learn new things to be different than you are. You must be willing to look in order to see what you are searching for. Take action to bring these things into existence. You can do all that the moment you give yourself permission and encourage yourself to walk in darkness. Your light will learn to shine, it will light your path, and you will discover the greatest treasures. You are your highest authority, and you are the most qualified person there will ever be to hold that position. Take responsibility and take action. The only wrong you can do for yourself is nothing.

You can do this. You can have the courage to embody the tenants I use:

1. Taking responsibility endows me with authority.
2. Accepting culpability enriches me with freedom.
3. My thoughts become my instructions.
4. My actions and inactions affect everything.
5. The truth provides me the strength to be competent and optimistic in my endeavor to be effectively benevolent.
6. I am venerated with an essential and unique contribution to the world.
7. My success is inextricably equitable to my proficiency of self. The quality of my life rises and falls with the quality of my character. I must always know who I am.

THE CATCH

It may seem too good to be true that something you just read in a few hours could catapult you into a remarkable life experience. Well, that's accurate. If you just read this and put it down, it won't be any different than any useful thing you have heard but never practiced. I can't hold your hand down the path; hell, I can hardly keep myself on it. There is no way I could know exactly how you are meant to traverse it. I marked the path from the entrance, described what to expect, and gave you navigation methods to stay abreast. It is imperative that you find your own way. Your way will be a little different from everyone else's. It must be different, or it's meaningless. If it's meaningless to you, it's worthless to the world. The difference in who you are will become the way you make a difference.

This path is dark, challenging, and has no finish line. I hope by now you know that's precisely why it's the one you want and have always been searching for. I hope you now believe in yourself enough to walk it instead of being seduced onto a path of empty promises and lies.

There is something called the "backward law." The observation of this law dates back to the Tao Te Ching, an ancient Chinese text written around the 4th century BC. The Tao is one of the oldest existential and philosophical writings known. So, this law has been with us since the beginning and still proves true. I have formulated this law into the previous methods and concepts described. So, even if this part confuses you, don't fret. You will likely adopt the proper thinking regardless. I do want to tell you how to break that law. Please remember, you don't have to completely know how something works to use it.

The law explains a tendency to become the method instead of the person using the method, which results opposite from one's original intention. It is possible to accidentally become the concept instead of the being who is considering the concept to use it. For example, suppose you get overly caught up in identifying with an idea such as improving yourself. In that case, you end up in a state of wanting to improve yourself constantly, which is like entering into a perpetual state of lacking. You are then trapped at zero in your experience. You will never be the improved person; as far as you know, you will always be the person trying to improve.

If you start defining yourself as the person trying to accomplish the things in this book, you will live stuck in that idea and could go nowhere, at least as far as your experience is concerned. Here is a warning, however; you must use this kind of book like a raft that gets you across a river, as Buddha said about dharma in "The Parable of the Raft." While you are on the raft (this book), you are aware of it. Still, when you get to the other side of the river, you must get off the raft and continue your journey. You cannot stay on the raft and expect to step foot on the other side. And there is no need to carry your raft after that. You will have to abandon this book and the idea that you need it.

Here is how to break the backward law.

You can't grasp for the results you want. You should imagine them and feel them in your vision. You must focus more on the quality of what you are doing instead of the reasons why and trust in what will come of it. Conversely and ironically, it's essential to have a bigger reason for why we do things other than only their individually beneficial results. The answer to dissolving that paradox is to have a higher purpose than yourself as your fundamental reason for improving. You must bring everyone with you in some way.

I dropped hints throughout this text suggesting that the highest level of obtainment from these initiatives will always be the disposition, ability, and desire to be a benevolent force of some kind. Benevolent meaning organized for the purpose of doing good. Most of us confuse compassion with benevolence. We can be uselessly compassionate. And maybe that isn't the worst thing, but it isn't the same as being powerfully benevolent.

Useless, compassionate people usually do little other than make a lot of noise to try to force others to make improvements. Groups of people like this are a destructive force to free societies. It leads to enacting believed improvements that become deterioration because the authors were incompetent and ill-informed. It can deteriorate further into using their perceived compassion as some shield against criticism, so the problem persists. Then, they weaponize their imagined virtue and turn it into an ideology that people must be indoctrinated into because no one would otherwise come to believe things that aren't true or useful. On the other hand, useful, compassionate people have a genuine interest and ability to improve societies and communities. So, they seek the truth and how to actually do something helpful.

You want to be among those who actually do something good outside themselves. Focusing only on being compassionate doesn't get you there. Compassion floats on a cloud of softness. Benevolence stands on a pyramid of honesty, strength, and fortitude. You can have both, but don't confuse them. Your compassion may motivate you to do good at best, but your benevolence enables you to do so in any circumstance. The moment things become terrible, compassion dissipates, and the only people left holding things together are those who are strong and able.

"Be not simply good- be good for something." – Henry David Thoreau.

A person must have himself in order before offering much value outside himself. This is the bigger reason why we are making these profound improvements to ourselves, even if we can't see it yet. We enjoy the successes, and that's okay. That is where the attractive value resides. The bigger reason you are doing things to better yourself will lead you forward instead of into the backward law: only if the reason is to become properly organized for the purpose of doing good.

That doesn't mean you must constantly be on a crusade to help others. Instead, you will incidentally be helping others and the world through your actions and example. Furthermore, you will always be positioned and able to help people intentionally, especially in the worst circumstances. You will quickly find that people will not always herald positive attention and gratitude to you for doing so and that's okay. Most of the best ways to help make things better are things some people won't like at the moment, such as telling the unpopular truth to useless, compassionate people seeking to infringe their errors upon our society. This is where you need something stronger than compassion.

Also, the most harmful thing you could do for someone is steal their discomfort, struggles, and obstacles. You are stealing their growth, self-reliance, confidence, etc. They must walk their own path. You can show them the truth, the light, and the way, and you can show them love. You can encourage them. You can be present with them, so they don't feel alone. Those things are true compassion, but they won't steal their victories. Lead them to victory the way you have come.

You can identify with improving and strengthening yourself to be a powerful benevolent force as much as you want, and it will never take you into the backward law so long as you are being honest and seeking the truth.

You will never surpass the deeply rewarding quality of how it feels to be someone everyone around you can count on for real. This is especially true because, by necessity, you must first become the person you can count on and will feel that in every moment. You will feel it in your persona, thoughts, consciousness, body, and dreams. Then, pass this book on to someone else.